1978-2008
CHINA EMERGING

How Thinking about Business Changed

WU XIAOBO

Translated by Martha Avery

图书在版编目（CIP）数据

中国巨变：1978 ~ 2008 = China Emerging: 1978–2008/ 吴晓波著；
（美）艾梅霞（Avery, M.）译 .—北京：五洲传播出版社，2008.7
ISBN 978-7-5085-1363-8
I. 中 ...
II. ①吴 ... ②艾 ...
III. 改革开放－历史－中国－ 1978 ~ 2008 －英文
IV. D61
中国版本图书馆 CIP 数据核字 (2008) 第 065084 号

Chief Advisor ╱ Wang Chen
Chief Planner ╱ Li Bing
Chief Supervisor ╱ Guo Changjian
Publisher ╱ Li Xiangping
Chief Editor ╱ Wu Wei

China Emerging: 1978–2008
How Thinking about Business Changed

Author ╱ Wu Xiaobo
Photo Credit ╱ www.sohu.com China Foto Press China Intercontinental Press
　　　　　　　　Blue Lion Publishing Center Oriental Morning Post
Executive Editor ╱ Deng Jinhui
Contributing Editor ╱ Pan Yue
Art Directors ╱ Tian Lin & Fu Xiaobin
Designer ╱ Beijing Primary Colors Design Co.
Publishers ╱ China Intercontinental Press
　　　　　　　(6 Beixiaomachang, Lianhuachi Donglu, Haidian District, Beijing, China)
　　　　　　　China CITIC Press
　　　　　　　(13th Floor, Coal Tower, 35 Block 13, Heping Jie, Chaoyang District, Beijing, China)
Printer ╱ Beijing C&C Joint Printing Co., Ltd.
Edition ╱ July 2008, 1st edition, 1st print run
Format ╱ 787mm x 1092mm 1/16
Signatures ╱ 12.75
Words ╱ 100,000
Print Run ╱ 1– 5,000
Price ╱ RMB 72.00 *yuan*

TABLE OF CONTENTS

Preface /1

1 The Beginning: 1978–1983 /3

Deng Opens the Door to the World /4
Where Will the Money Come from? /15
Shenzhen Special Economic Zone /21
Reform at Capital Steel /27
Shooting Stars in the Countryside /34

2 Commotion and Tumult: 1984–1992 /41

1984, the "Founding Year" of Major Chinese Enterprises /42
A Two-track Pricing Policy and a Trip to Hainan Island /52
Allowing Prices to "Break through the Pass" /63
"Harnessing and Rectifying" /69

3 Radical Dreams: 1993–1997 /83

Ruling over Chaos with an "Iron Wrist" /85
Price Wars /97
Becoming One of the Fortune 500 /103
Unexpected Changes /111

4 Swamps and Landmines: 1998–2002 /119

Some Hairpins /120
The Birthing of the Stock Market, and Its Chronic Problems /129
Stride on over the Rainbow /138
The China Threat /147

5 Responsibility and Reason: 2003–2008 /153

SARS, Housing Bubbles, Electricity Panics /154
Trade Frictions /162
Internet Economics /176
Great Nation Passion /184
Crossroads /191

Acknowledgments /196

PREFACE

I am always amazed by the power of perceptions, that is, by the power of what people perceive things to be. History is a succession of mental images linked by time. Years later, when people recall an era, what float to mind are those images, those classic moments.

My intenet in writing this book has been to extract certain moments and present them as key to what happened over this past thirty years in China. Over the last four years I have written two volumes that narrate China's evolving reality from a business or commercial perspective. This book is a condensed version of those two volumes—I have reduced 700,000 words down to 60,000 and added 250 photographs.

The thirty years from 1978 to 2008 have marked a period of rapid economic ascent for China. China's abrupt emergence may indeed be the most notable phenomenon in global economics for these decades. Today, as I thumb through the photographs, I am yet again astonished at the changes in China—the photos tell the story no less starkly than the text. I say to myself, "Is this really the same China? Did we really do this?" From the photo of blood-red fingerprints of farmers at Xiaogang Village, pressed onto a document declaring their determination, I read the distress and the resolve of ordinary people. From the image of students at Tian'anmen unfurling a banner that says with such gladness, "Hello Xiaoping!" I can almost hear the welcoming shout of history. From a very indistinct photo of Zhang Ruimin smashing refrigerators—for my assistant and I could not find any better copy—I see with

absolute clarity the moment when the bones of young Chinese entrepreneurs started growing. And from the crazily happy smile on people's faces, I wonder at the phenomenal force behind change.

A Japanese photographer whom I admire, Ogawa Shinsuke, has said that when the most explosive events of history erupt, individuals are always propelling those events behind the scenes. This catches the reality underlying China's recent thirty years. China's changes have been the work of individual people, and have been based on "the freedom-inspired creativity of the Chinese people." The person attesting to this has been none other than China's current Premier, Wen Jiabao.

Oswald Spengler too noted, in *The Decline of the West*, that individuals perform the duties arranged by the inevitable forces of history. Those who are willing participants lead the way; those who are not willing are simply dragged along.

The past thirty years in China have this inherent quality of being inevitable. Events might have suffered some chance interruption, but the underlying necessity persisted, like an inextinguishable spirit.

Today, we call that spirit a "market economy."

Wu Xiaobo
2008, Hangzhou

PART ONE

The Beginning
1978–1983

Photograph of students of the class of '7811' of the Beijing Post and Telecommunications Institute.

Deng Opens the Door to the World

The winter of 1978 was particularly cold. A thin light came through the grayness of Beijing as a Xinhua News correspondent, using the most oblique innuendo, noted that the political situation was beginning to change. "A hint of sun is finally breaking through the coldness, bringing a small measure of warmth to people's lives. In this huge city, with its crowded apartments, its narrow checkerboard streets, the masses of people can begin to feel some relief."

1978 marked the start of China's momentous change. In this year China began to respond to the call of a different destiny. Ten years of the spasms of the Cultural Revolution and more than twenty years of a "planned economy" had put the country on the verge of collapse. There was exactly one bank in all of China. There was no insurance company, there were no financial institutions. Total reserves in the country came to RMB 108.99 billion, including those of State-owned enterprises and the central treasury. All of this was deposited in the one bank, making up 83.8% of the country's total sum of money. Fixed assets in any State-owned enterprise were paid for with "allocations" from the bank. Working capital came from loans from the bank.

In the twenty years between 1958 and 1978, the average income per year of people in towns and cities increased by less than RMB 4. The average income per year of farmers increased by less than RMB 2.6. To avoid exposing heavy industry to bombing in the event of war, China's industries had been put, not in the economically advantageous position along the coast, but far in the interior, the "rear defense" of the country. Contrary to any kind of rational economic decision-making, important industry was placed in mountainous regions where transport costs were high. Intentionally dispersed at a great distance from each other, factories forfeited any advantage from proximity or economies of scale. Efficiency was extremely low in all industries but light industry in particular was crippled. People used State-issued coupons for grain and daily necessities.

The situation could scarcely continue. Prospects for the country were extremely grim. In 1978, a tiny giant of a man, Deng Xiaoping, stepped onto the stage of history for a second time. He began to guide China's reconstruction and to pick up the beat as he steered the country in the direction of wholesale change. He had astonishing determination, extreme political astuteness, and absolute decisiveness.

Deng Xiaoping was elected Chairman of the CPPCC, or Chinese People's Political Consultative Conference, in March of 1978 at the first meeting of its fifth session. Shortly afterwards, he convened a "National Science Conference"

Left: The train station at Yongdingmen in Beijing in 1981.

Right: In the late 1970s and early 1980s, young couples could receive a voucher to purchase furniture when they registered to get married. With this in hand, they had to wait all night in line in order to buy one piece of furniture. This photograph, taken in the summer of 1980, shows a newly married couple returning home with their furniture.

Deng Xiaoping was made Chairman of the Chinese People's Political Consultative Conference in March 1978. This implied his formal rehabilitation.

at which 6,000 attendees were astonished and delighted to hear him say that "science and technology are the primary productive force," and that "intellectuals too are part of the workers' class." This was unheard of in a country where, two years earlier, intellectuals were still being persecuted. At this meeting, the leaders of the country acknowledged that China was fifteen to twenty years behind the rest of the world in many areas. They now proposed a stirring plan for the development of science. By the end of the twentieth century, Chinese science was to "catch up with and overtake" the level of science in the rest of the world. This unfeasible goal was not realized, but it served the purpose of arousing the entire country. All Chinese now heard the unmistakable screech of a train switching tracks.

Any major change in history must be preceded by a change in people's conceptual framework. After a full ten years of the Cultural Revolution, all normal functioning of the country had been destroyed, including people's ability to think creatively and clearly.

An awarded certificate issued by the National Science Conference, which showed that 'the springtime of science' had arrived.

The trial of the 'Gang of Four,' on November 20, 1980. From left, Zhang Chunqiao, Wang Hongweng, Yao Wenyuan, and Jiang Qing.

People's minds were in the rigid grip of what was called "extreme leftist thinking." For many years, the country had been closed to outside information, "locked up," which affected the psychological makeup of its population. This now began to change as official indications of the shift in policy appeared in newspapers. On May 11, the *Guangming Daily* published a "special editorial" entitled, "Actual Experience Is the Only Standard for Judging Truth." This was then picked up and republished by the government's Xinhua News Agency. On the following day the official Communist Party organ, the *People's Daily*, published the full text. The author of the piece stated that "any theory that supercedes reality and declares itself to be inviolable and not open to questioning is not scientific, and is not truly Marxism-Leninism, or Maoist Thought. Instead, it is obscurantism, blind idealism, cultural authoritarianism." The article caused a national sensation. Several days later, Deng Xiaoping officially confirmed the new line by saying that the thinking was in line with Marxism and Leninism. He called upon everyone to "cast off the shackles that bind our spirit," and said, "We need to bring about a great emancipation in our way of thinking."

This new approach to the standard by which one evaluates truth was to permeate the entire course of China's reform.

It obliterated the old political principal known in shorthand as the "two all of's." The new thinking was quite different. In terms of economics, it aimed to set up a whole new conceptual framework and attitude toward business. This attitude toward the "ethics" or acceptability of doing business strongly influences China's reforms to this day.

By summer 1978, people witnessed another powerful indication of the momentum for change. The college entrance examination system had been partially restored in 1977, but the first comprehensive exam in over ten years was held in 1978. Over 6.1 million people rushed to qualify for a position in a school. Many were no longer young. In the 1960s and 1970s, many had been forced to take part in a political movement that sent them out to towns and villages in the countryside to work on a long-term and indeed indefinite basis. This movement was a result of lack of employment in cities and represented the government's attempt to disperse a large urban labor pool to the countryside. People were now frantic to leave farming communities and have a new chance in life. Out of the millions taking the exam, only 400,000 were selected to enter schools. The fates of those

1. Deng Xiaoping visited Japan in 1978, and took a ride on the Shinkansen high-speed train.

2. China reinstituted the exam for entry into institutions of higher education in 1977. This photograph shows an examination hall in Beijing. The slogan behind says, 'In order to realize the Four Modernizations...'

3. Deng Xiaoping among college students.

GLOSSARY

Two all of's

After the "Gang of Four" was "pulverized" as the Chinese put it in October 1976, a man named Hua Guofeng became the highest leader in the country and he immediately declared his support for this "two all of's" principle. It stood for the following motto: "All of Chairman Mao's policies are correct and we will resolutely follow them; all of Chairman Mao's instructions are correct and we will be unwavering in obeying them."

Deng Xiaoping and President Carter, waving from the terrace of the White House on January 31, 1979.

who were chosen changed radically. Today, many of the outstanding students from that initial class are senior government officials and China's premier businessmen.

After successfully initiating a national debate about this "standard for judging truth," Deng Xiaoping made a historic trip to Japan. Deng had studied abroad in France in his youth, and had worked in a printing plant. For over half a century, however, he had not set foot inside a "capitalist" factory. He left China on October 22, and traveled first to Tokyo where he toured steel and automobile factories, then made a special trip to see Matsushita Electric where he met with the 83-year-old Konosuke Matsushita, founder of the company. The former Japanese Ambassador to China, Nakae Yosuke, who was present, recalled the occasion. Matsushita asked Deng Xiaoping what he might find of interest in Japan. Deng Xiaoping replied that Chinese winters were extremely cold, and people had to burn coal briquets to stay warm with the result that they often fell prey to carbon monoxide poisoning. He wondered if Japan had briquets that did not produce carbon monoxide.

Other momentous changes occurred in 1978. One that is often overlooked is that the Chinese government stopped its aid to Vietnam on July 3, 1978. Thirteen days later, China went on to announce that it was canceling all economic and technical

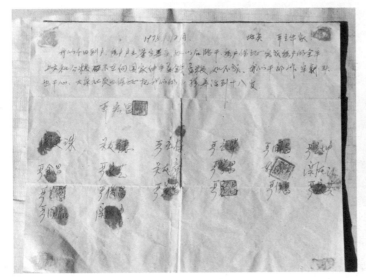

assistance to Albania. On October 23, the Sino-Japanese Peace Accords formally went into effect, and on December 16, 1978, a Sino-American Communiqué was issued, establishing normal diplomatic relations. Many more subtle changes in foreign policy indicated that China had begun to disengage from ideological considerations and put its national policy focus squarely on economic development.

All of these major political changes were centered on Beijing, but in fact the most significant economic event of 1978 occurred not in a city but in an extremely backwards, isolated, and impoverished village. On the evening of November 24, a group of twenty-one yellow-skinned, gaunt farmers crouched around the dim light of a kerosene lamp in a small thatch-roofed hut. They met in secret, in a village called the Xiaogang Production Brigade of Fengyang County, Anhui Province. Their faces were haggard, they wore old rags, but they were solemn and dignified as they pressed their fingers into red ink and then placed their fingerprints on a document before them. Each man swore that he would rather go to jail or be killed than carry on under the existing system. They agreed to split up the fields by household and cultivate the plots on their own. This agreement was later to be placed in the Museum of Chinese Revolution (now part of the National Museum of China) for safekeeping. It

Left: On November 24, 1978, a group of farmers in the Xiaogang Production Brigade in Fengyang County, Anhui Province, secretly signed their 'handprints' to a document committing them to a '*chengbao*' responsibility system as a way of farming their collective land. This system allowed individuals to farm plots of land separately and to keep what was left over after allocations to the State. 'We hand over to the State the required allocation, the collective retains what has been produced beyond the allocation, and the individual is allowed to keep what is left over.'

Right: The first group of farmers to undertake individual tending of their own plots. China's agricultural reforms were said to be 'born out of their hands.' They are Yan Junchang, Yan Lixue, and Yan Likun, standing before the plots on which they practised the '*cheng-bao*' or contract system.

The bountiful harvest in 1982 after the '*da-bao-gan*' system was put into effect.

is considered the "first shot" in China's agricultural reform.

Before 1978, the People's Commune System had tied farmers securely to the ground for more than twenty years. The shortcomings of a system that mandated "one big pot for everyone" were grimly apparent. As a result, the productivity of agriculture fell to a point where farmers were simply no longer able to survive. Xiaogang Village was known as a "village of three dependencies:" it depended on government subsidies of grain for food, on financial assistance for common necessities, and on loans for inputs into ongoing production. Practically every family in the village had to go out into neighboring regions to beg for food after every fall harvest. Drought conditions in the spring of 1978 greatly reduced that year's grain harvests. With no alternative, the farmers of Xiaogang Village took matters into their own hands. They instituted a system, '*da-bao-gan*,' whereby each family became responsible for its own part of the village production. Some payment came in crops and some in cash. In the next year, Xiaogang produced a bumper harvest and for the first time handed "public grain" on up to the government as well as paid off some of its debt. With the strong support of Wan Li, the First Secretary of Anhui Provincial Party Committee at

GLOSSARY

Da-guo-fan

Or "one big pot." Under the "one big pot" system, everyone received the same amount irrespective of the benefits that his work created. Everyone ate from the same "big pot" of the State.

the time, the example of Xiaogang Village was then promoted throughout Anhui as the model to follow. This system, named the "Household Contract Responsibility System," is generally acknowledged as having been the precipitating event for change in villages throughout China.

Looking back over the course of China's thirty years of reform, we discover that often the most important changes were instigated by the people themselves. Policy makers have found that their task was to understand how to "go with the flow" and enhance the end result. In addition to having the necessary courage and spirit, they simply had to figure out how to channel the people's own creativity along the correct path.

Another remarkable discovery, in looking back thirty years, is the recognition of just how far removed China was from the rest of the world and how far it had to go to catch up. At a time when the penetration rate of televisions in the US market was over 70%, in China it was near zero. Only in July of 1978 did the *People's Daily* allow the first advertisement in its pages; from August onward, the paper would occasionally publish the very limited television programming schedule. The government still encouraged extreme frugality among people, especially with regard to old cement bags—they were to be reused and never thrown away. In 1978, a person from Beijing traveled to Shanghai and saw that in a bookstore window they were touting their "open-shelf" system: people could actually go in and browse for books instead of buying them at a distance with a broad counter and a forbidding employee in between. As someone was later to say, "If we had known just

Left: Chinese tourists in the summer of 1980. The foreigners are the main attraction, not the Summer Palace or the national treasures. In 1978, a tourist group in Lanzhou was surrounded and stared at by 100,000 astonished Lanzhou residents.

Right: Pierre Cardin walked down Chang'an Street in Beijing in March of 1978. Cardin was the first world-class fashion designer to come to China.

The Third Plenary Session of the Eleventh Central Committee of the Communist Party of China in December 1978. This is the famous meeting that 'drew aside the curtain on the era of reform and opening up.'

how far apart we were from the world back in 1978, I don't know if we would have had the courage to press on."

Change now began to accelerate. From December 18 to 22, 1978, one of the most important meetings in modern Chinese history took place in Beijing, the Third Plenary Session of the Eleventh Central Committee of the Communist Party of China. The sole topic of this meeting was, "Shifting the Focus of All Party Work toward Socialist Modernization and Construction." Parsing that phrase was part of the work of the meeting. The assembly agreed to stop using the slogans, "Take class struggle as the guiding principle," and "Carry on revolution under the dictatorship of the proletariat." It re-established the structure and "line" of the Party. It opposed any tendency to adulate one person and propagandize

An ad from the *Shanghai Pictorial* of 1982, for the Feiyue Television.

about him. It evaluated and overturned false accusations against certain people that had been made in the course of the past few years and looked at problems regarding "contributions and mistakes" by senior leaders. It was a meeting of tremendous symbolic significance, implying that, from now on, "politicized life" would no longer be the basic mode of existence for the Chinese people. Instead, China had returned to the world stage and to an arena of peaceful competition. From now on, having survived one hundred years of extreme political turbulence, this Asian country would be using economic development as the means to move towards a better tomorrow.

Time magazine selected Deng Xiaoping as 'Man of the Year,' and put him on the cover of the magazine on January 1, 1979. Deng and China began to attract the world's attention.

China's doors were opening and her people were suddenly looking on all that was "Outside" with great wonder and interest. China and the world had been cut off from each other for so long that the West too was hyper-curious about a place that seemed different from everywhere else. At the end of 1978, Deng Xiaoping was put on the cover of *Time* magazine for the second time, the first time being after Premier Zhou Enlai died in 1976. Not only was Deng chosen as "Man of the Year," but the magazine devoted 48 pages to describing him and the newly reopened China. The headline with which *Time* began the article was, "Visions of a New China."

Children and foreigners strolling in front of Tian'anmen, the Gate of Heavenly Peace, Beijing.

Where Will the Money Come from?

"Starting is always the hardest part." This Chinese saying was certainly appropriate to a man who was intending to undertake a full-scale reconstruction of China. The first question he faced: where is all the money going to come from?

In 1978, China's total foreign exchange reserves came to the

Take a photo with the car. A scene of the Forbidden City and a Red Flag auto in 1980, at the very early stages of a still-uncertain market economy.

trivial amount of USD 167 million. Thirty years later, in 2008, China's foreign exchange reserves exceed USD 1.7 trillion. The total has increased more than ten-thousand times. Unlike Mao Zedong who mobilized the populace for economic construction, Deng intended to mobilize capital. He planned to call upon the money of capitalism to create "China's mighty edifice."

His first step was to hold discussions with working members of the Central Committee of the Communist Party. In these discussions he pointed out, "It is altogether acceptable to expand business with overseas partners, to do, say, some 50 billion. Be a little braver, stride out a little further. Don't keep debating things forever, getting all the details right before you start. In terms of industries, set up factories and operations as fast as possible in coal, ferrous metals, oil, electric power plants, electronics, weapons, transportation, communications, even feedstocks." Few people realize that, based on these discussions, the Central Government formulated a massive ten-year plan for attracting USD 60 billion of foreign investment, in order to expand industry, agriculture, science and technology, and weapons production. The plan included 120 large-scale projects, including mines, petrochemical plants, and steel refineries.

For a long time after these discussions, the government's primary responsibility became to attract foreign business and foreign investment. In a book called *The Building of Modern China*, author Peng Min revealed that, in 1978 alone, agreements were signed for more than USD 7.8 billion. Of this amount, around half were signed in just ten days, from December 20 to the end of 1978.

In August of 1978, the First Machinery Industry Ministry in charge of the automobile industry in China issued telegrams inviting General Motors, Ford, Toyota, Nissan, Reynault, Citroen, Benz, Volkswagon and others to China, hoping that they would come quickly to investigate the "China market."

The first to come was General Motors. On October

Young people selling bowls of tea in front of the Wumen Gate of the Forbidden City. One large bowl cost 2 *fen* (RMB cent). There was little selection in beverages back then and tea was sold everywhere.

The earliest production line for Santana cars in Shanghai. For nearly fifteen years, Santana was the most popular car in China.

21, a large delegation led by Thomas A. Murphy came to discuss potential projects. Li Lanqing, the future Vice premier, received them, and later recalled how Murphy mentioned the concept of a "joint venture." He asked why the Chinese seemed interested only in importing technology, and not in setting up a joint venture.

Li Lanqing later told CCTV reporters that although the Chinese people understood English and knew the words "joint" and "venture," which must have to do with "mutually shouldering risk," they were very hazy about any details.

Shortly after this, a delegation from Volkswagon came to Shanghai. The delegation met with leaders to discuss a potential joint venture for producing Volkswagon cars. These discussions were to last a full ten years and the only thing the Chinese side insisted was that Volkswagon had to localize.

Meanwhile, multinational companies did begin to enter China. In the year 1979, the first batch of 3,000 boxes of Coca-Cola departed from Hong Kong, bound for Beijing. After test marketing, the US side signed an agreement that included the donation of a bottling plant to the COFCO (China National Cereals, Oils and Foodstuffs Corp.) that could fill 300 bottles of Coca-Cola a minute. The ten-year agreement gave exclusive license to COFCO to use the Coca-Cola brand and

The first shipment of Coca-Cola arrives in Beijing, September 1979.

produce and sell product on the Mainland.

One amusing sequel to this story is that COFCO wanted to erect the plant in Shanghai at the same location as a historic soda-bottling plant, Aquarius Company, that had been established in 1864. Shanghai resolutely opposed this. The charge against COFCO was that it was selling out the country, acting as a slave to Westerners, and importing the decadent lifestyle of the capitalist class. It was also undermining the nation's own industry. As a result, COFCO set up the factory in Fengtai outside Beijing. The production initially supplied tourist hotels, but this market was quickly saturated and, after getting permission from the Ministry of Commerce, from 1982 onward the excess Coca-Cola was sold in the markets of Beijing.

At the same general time, China began to loosen restrictions on foreign journalists in the country. A journalist for the *Nihon Keizai Shimbun* named Okada was soon reporting that China's flights were always being cancelled. Another Japanese journalist visited a steel plant in Chongqing and discovered to his amazement that it was still using a 140-year-old British-made steam-roller in its processing. Jay Matthews, a journalist of the *Washington Post*, turned heaven and earth in order to get permission to visit a State-run factory in Guilin. He reported, "As in most factories in China, workers at this Guilin silk factory

Textile workers in the Number Two Textile Factory in Shanghai take a lesson from their older colleagues in 1982. For twenty years, the female textile workers in Shanghai and the male workers at the Daqing Oil Field were the 'model workers' for the rest of the country.

are not putting much effort into their work." He then stated categorically, "This relaxed work attitude is going to be a major obstacle to the modernization of this most populous nation on earth." The far-sighted British magazine, the *Economist*, predicted in one article that for the immediate future China would be importing equipment and that this would stimulate production in industrially advanced countries. Looking to the longer term, however, "a ferocious flood of Chinese exports is going to be the necessary consequence." Twenty years later, this forecast certainly came true.

For both sides, nothing was as smooth and easy as people expected. Foreign investors soon discovered that the policy environment in China was turbulent and opaque and also that, given the extreme backwardness of its basic infrastructure, China was not an ideal place in which to invest. A German correspondent of *Der Spiegel* who had accompanied a

A labor union card from 1979.

Volkswagon delegation wrote with a certain derision in his voice, "Volkswagon will be operating on a kind of island. There are virtually no spare parts suppliers here, and China's methods of production all date from my grandfather's era." The American businessman Charles Abrams was the first to feel the shock of cold water. In a 1980 issue of *Fortune* magazine, he was still being described as "a successful representative of the new American dream of going to China to strike it rich." A fifty-seven year-old real estate salesman in New York, Abrams set up a trading company and proceeded to visit China over forty times. His conclusion was that China was like one big company. He was received warmly by Chinese officials and was able to get "white papers" from many State-owned enterprises, even initial orders and contracts worth tens of millions. On this basis he successfully raised USD 25 million in financing on the New York stock exchange. Many of the contracts he had in hand turned to useless pieces of paper in the course of the next year, however. A China expert at Harvard University, John King Fairbank, was soon to say, "Importing USD 60 million worth of projects in one year is not a realistic goal. Within around a year, China is going to have to reduce it dramatically. Many contracts that were signed will be cancelled or postponed, because China simply lacks the ability to pay."

As soon as Deng Xiaoping discovered that this plan was impossible to execute, he swiftly changed course. He now placed his emphasis on reforming the hundreds of thousands of State-owned enterprises, hoping that productivity would be stimulated by granting them more autonomy. At the same time, he began an experiment in "Special Economic Zones" in southern China, geographically remote from the center in Beijing and where State-owned economic forces were weakest. He used this "window effect" to attract foreign capital and technology.

The road between Guangzhou and Shenzhen in 1982, with the signs, 'To Shekou' and 'To Guangzhou.' At the time, these were highly tempting signposts.

Shenzhen Special Economic Zone

In the springtime of 1979, therefore, a small fishing village on the South China Sea coastline adjoining Hong Kong was thrust into historical prominence. You could not have found its name on any map before this. Nobody imagined that this tiny place would soon become the most vital "economic engine" in China.

On behalf of this place, Deng Xiaoping invented a new term, "Special Economic Zone." The crux of the concept was that such a Zone took precedence in terms of policies. In fact, as early as the end of 1978, Deng Xiaoping had declared that it was all right to "let some cities get rich first." Not many people took note at the time that, when he mentioned a dozen names, the first on the list was a place called Shenzhen. Shenzhen was separated from the most capitalistic city on earth by one small river. For Deng Xiaoping to choose this place to serve as a "breakthrough in opening" was undeniably taking new risks. It was also another instance of his "feeling for the rocks with your feet as you cross the river." The idea of Special Economic Zones signified that he was beginning to explore a path of "gradual reform with Chinese characteristics," of choosing the lesser of two evils. Since "heaven is high and the emperor far away," the coastal areas of the southeast were far removed from the interior and only weakly influenced by the planned economy. The feeling was that even if the experiment failed, it would not be a major problem.

Shenzhen's tremendous changes have provided a lively background to the dramatic stories of early migrants to this place, people from all over China who came to make their fortunes.

When the region was first given permission to become a Special Economic Zone, the State allocated a sum of RMB 30 million towards its development. This amount was hardly enough to develop two square kilometers, while Shenzhen at the time measured fifty kilometers from east to west and included a total of 327.5 square kilometers. "Three-connects and one-leveling" are the conventional way of reckoning development costs in China: connecting water, electricity, and roads, and leveling the land. In order to pay for these "three-connects and one-leveling," Shenzhen thought of a better way than government allocations: it would turn land into money. On January 1, 1980, land-use rights for first piece of land in Shenzhen were leased for money. This was widely considered to be "selling out the country" at the time. Finally someone found a reference in Lenin's *Collected Works* that referred to the conditions under which leasing might be considered acceptable. "…During the transition period, it is not absolutely necessary for housing, factories, and so on to be handed over to individuals or cooperatives for their use without any payment in return. At the same time, eliminating a private system of ownership of land does not require eliminating leasing of land. It merely requires that the form of land use is changed in a way that continues to transmit the benefits to society." Cadres in Shenzhen at the time could recite this line by heart. In 1982, the founder of the Shekou Special Economic Zone in Shenzhen named Yuan Geng erected a massive plate at the gate of the Management Commission of Shekou. "Time is money. Efficiency is your lifeline." The plate's motto traveled swiftly throughout China to become the iconic phrase of change in China.

Party Secretary of Guangdong Province, Ren Zhongyi (left), receives a report from Yuan Geng (squatting in the middle) at Shekou, Shenzhen, in June of 1982.

Leasing land brought with it an endless stream of wealth, and Hong Kong businessmen were the first to taste its sweetness. Land-use fees in Shenzhen were roughly one-eleventh the price of land across the river in Hong Kong. Shenzhen used this money to level hills, fill in valleys, start postal services, and build roads, electric power lines, and water mains. From 1980 to 1985, Shenzhen's "actually used" foreign investment totaled RMB 1.28 billion. The Zone completed infrastructure investment totalling RMB 7.63 billion in investment, it built a number of basic infrastructure projects in resources, transportation, and telecommunications, and the beginnings of nine industrial regions. Hong Kong businessmen poured into the Zone to start companies and open factories. The "south wind" wafted northward from this thriving area, and soon the power of "opening" could no longer be restrained.

'Time is money. Efficiency is your lifeline.' This motto, which appeared first in Shekou, shocked many people and overturned long-held concepts.

With the appearance of Shenzhen and other Special Economic

Zones, large amounts of both capital and human talent began to flow towards China's southeast. This movement spawned the strange offspring of a changing economic system, namely opportunists who were adept in what is called "reselling" in Chinese. They took advantage of disparities in two co-existing economic structures. They were called "Masters of the art of reselling," or "*dao-ye*" in Chinese. Their senses were highly attuned to market prices and to those nebulous areas of the changing system that were still undefined by laws or regulations. This "grey" territory allowed them to carry on all kinds of rent-seeking activities. In cultivating official connections, they tripped lightly between Beijing and Shenzhen, and stories of overnight fortunes became common. In the end, like swarms of carpenter ants, these people chewed through the rigid restrictions that had bound the distribution system of a planned economy until it was left in tatters. People might disparage them and envy their wealth, but they played a very useful function.

Small-scale private business was just beginning in 1982, and the girl selling clothes was leery of being photographed.

In short time, taking its cue from these Masters, Shenzhen became the Supreme Headquarters in buying and selling for the entire country. Senior officials of inland provinces came to set up trading companies in Shenzhen, using its special privileges to carry out "reselling" directly. Dr. Thomas Chan of the Centre of Asian Studies, Hong Kong University, studied the phenomenon of Shenzhen and discovered that, by 1983, when Yuan Geng and others were espousing four "Shenzhen development goals," these had already *de facto* been shoved to one side. They were, first, "In products, exports are primary," but in fact imports exceeded exports by USD 484 million. Second, "Importing advanced technology is primary," but in fact any imported technology was mainly old equipment that had been discarded by Hong Kong and Japan. Third, "Foreign investment is primary," while in fact the ratio of foreign to local investment was only 30%, and most of the foreign investment came from Hong Kong. Fourth, "In terms of economic structure, industrial development is primary," but in 1983 Shenzhen's industrial production totaled RMB 720 million while the retail value of consumer items that passed through the Zone was RMB 1.25 billion. The money made from trading far exceeded any money made from industry.

Although the abrupt rise of Shenzhen did not conform to what was intended, its effectiveness as a model for others is indisputable. Later, whenever the economy ran into uncomfortable volatility, people could always pin the problems on Shenzhen. The implication was that this "extreme frontline" in China's progress was perhaps moving too fast. When inflation picked up in 1985 and China began its first round of "macro-economic adjustments" by tightening money supply, the ramifications for Shenzhen were severe. Years later, Ren Zhongyi, who had served as First Secretary of Guangdong Provincial Party Committee, was to say, "Guangdong has had to fight its way along a bloody path, for the pressure on it has been intense. Back then, Guangdong was expected to lead the way in 'feeling out' the future, but it was also expected to bear the brunt of all resulting criticism. The Guangdong Provincial Party Committee simply kept on track. It never deviated from the intent to open China to the outside world."

The basic cellular mechanisms of China's economy began to regenerate in 1979. All kinds of modern economic factors began to revive. In March, China established the State Administration of Foreign Exchange, responsible for overseeing all matters to do with foreign exchange transactions. China's Enterprise Management Association was established in the same year; CCTV set up its first advertising department which, twenty years later, had become China's most powerful ad agency. On May 1, 1979, the old-time Peking Duck restaurant named "Quanjude" reopened. In Shanghai, some former businessmen and a few overseas Chinese raised funds for an enterprise called the "Shanghai Municipal Industrial and Commercial Patriotic Construction Company." Later this was recognized as being the first "people-operated enterprise" in China. The first advertising company also appeared in this city that had long since enjoyed more than one hundred years of commercial traditions. On March 15, 1979, Shanghai's paper, the *Wenhui Bao*, published the first advertisement for the Swiss watch company RADO. On the same day, Shanghai Television put out its first television ads, for RADO. The ad was broadcast in English with Chinese subtitles. Although few could understand it, within three days more than seven hundred buyers had asked about the RADO watch in the department store of Huangpu District.

"Will China walk a capitalist road?" The Hong Kong economist Steven N.S. Cheung wrote presciently in 1979, "I predict that in time China will adopt an ownership structure that is akin to private ownership. I can state categorically that in the future China will allow to a considerable degree 'usage-rights' and 'transfer-rights' for such things as labor, means of production, buildings, even land." In a footnote to this article, he added that even though China in the future would allow transfer of resources and private use rights, China would perhaps never describe its economic system as being "capitalist" or one that allowed "private ownership." Ten years later, he became noted for the near-accuracy of his predictions. In around the year 2000, the noun "privately-held property" became a publicly recognized term in China. In 2004, the legal protection or legitimacy of the right to privately held assets was formally written into the Constitution of the People's Republic of China.

China's course of reform has followed many twists and turns. Setbacks are encountered by any large country as it develops, but in China many of the consequences have been unexpected. Whenever reform has encountered problems, all kinds of contradictions, both new and old, have come to the fore, allowing history to make various "adjustments." Overall, however, China's economy has shown remarkable regenerative power. The examples below suggest some of the obstacles that have been overcome.

The employees of a restaurant in Hangzhou on March 5, 1983, which was the twentieth anniversary of Mao Zedong's admonition to 'Study from Lei Feng.' The sign reads: 'Welcome to come sample our food, 4 grain coupons and 5 *jiao* (half of one RMB) per guest for fried rice with meat and vegetables and dessert.'

Reform at Capital Steel

A Hong Kong scholar took note of the following vignettes when he visited Guangzhou in 1979, details that gave him pause about the future of China. Two women were assigned to sweep leaves from an area outside his hotel window that measured a few hundred square meters. This was their entire responsibility, all day every day. At the same time, he noticed that it took three people to repair the plaster on a nearby wall. One held the bucket, another applied the plaster, and a third stood by to watch. Breakfast was said to be served for exactly one hour in the morning, but after half an hour the servers had quit. They sat in a corner of the room, chatting.

A watch factory and a television factory in Hangzhou, with the 'teams' ready to be 'of service.'

Low efficiency had always been a problem at State-owned enterprises in China since "everyone was boss while at the same time nobody took responsibility." While the planned

A privately operated book stall near a movie theater. Some two hundred people would come here daily to borrow books for a small fee, then bring them back and exchange them for others.

economy "ruled all under heaven," State-owned enterprises safely snuggled into the swaddling clothes of the State and were unconcerned about their own future. The State organized all production and all allocation of goods. The State set the prices of all goods and commodities. Any State-owned enterprise was merely a working unit under the planned-economy system. Leaders of enterprises were, in reality as well as in name, simply managers. On the one hand, such enterprises were clearly not equipped to face competition. On the other hand, State-owned enterprises held the economic lifeline of the country, were intimately tied to issues of social stability, and could not simply be done away with. They also embodied extremely complex personal relations among tiers of people so that reforming them was almost unimaginably difficult.

In order to resuscitate the deeply entrenched largest enter-

prises, the first prescription that policy makers considered was that of expanding their autonomy in decision-making. In May of 1979, the State Council announced that eight large State-owned

Popped rice was a favorite food when other snacks were not available; this photograph was taken in 1984 in Hangzhou.

Left: Many people hoped that their living conditions could be improved by having developers tear down their old homes and move them to new accommodations. There were too many to be moved, however, so that developers held back since there was no profit in it.

Right: A photography studio in Baxian County, Hebei Province, in January 1982. Long pigtails were considered unstylish by this time, so the girl was wearing a hat to look more fashionable.

enterprises would be first to engage in an experimental policy of expanded autonomy. The eight included Capital Steel, the Tianjin Bicycle Factory, and the Shanghai Diesel Engine Plant. In July, five documents were issued concurrently that expanded the decision-making power of these State-owned enterprises. Considerations related to increasing amortization rates, improving the use of depreciation allowances, modifying taxation on fixed assets, and turning disbursements of government funds for working capital into "credit loans" rather than simple "allocations." With these measures, the long journey of shaking up State-owned enterprises began. Countless numbers of economists were to spend sleepless nights over the problems and it was only years later that they came to the conclusion that the underlying crux of the problem had always been a clarification of ownership of assets. More years later, as China's economy surged ahead, the monopolistic position of certain State-owned enterprises enabled them to become China's most profitable companies.

Problems in reforming these enterprises in the early years quickly became apparent. Capital Steel employed over 200,000 people, but the head of the factory did not have the authority to "reform" a single toilet. In order to receive greater autonomy in decision-making, Capital Steel proposed the idea of what

北海公园快速冲卷卩

The Beihai Park in Beijing in 1980. Photograph developing technology had just come into the country, and young men and women could be seen everywhere checking newly developed films.

was called a *"cheng-bao"* or contract system. The factory guaranteed a basic amount of production to the State government, to fulfill its "Plan" requirements. Anything produced over that amount could be kept for its own account. Losses were to be carried by the factory as well as gains. In an era of extreme imbalance between supply and demand, when all goods were in short supply and everything a monopolistic factory produced could immediately be sold, fast growth of "reformed" enterprises was a foregone conclusion. As Capital Steel made more and more money, authorities began to demand more and more profits from it.

"Contradictions" between factory and State authorities, about who took what percentage, increased until they erupted in 1986. In December of that year, the Beijing Municipal Government issued an order to Capital Steel, saying it had to hand over a supplementary RMB 108.99 million in profit. Capital Steel refused to comply.

A fashionable youth who has not yet learned how to tie his new tie properly. Photographed in 1983.

December 28, 1978, at thirty degrees under zero, people lined up in the early morning to wait in line to buy alcohol with coupons. Each family was alloted coupons for two bottles of 'Jade Fountain' alcohol. This is in front of the Number Three Department Store at Heihe County, Heilongjiang Province. People swarmed in at around 8 am, when the doors cracked open. From the expression of the person who is looking back at the camera, one can get a sense of the rage and frustration at the extreme scarcity of goods back then.

Spring Festival (Chinese New Year) in 1986, at the same Department Store, but goods are becoming more abundant.

By 1998, the scene was totally different at this Department Store.

Instead, the head of the factory sent a letter directly to the State Council and to Deng Xiaoping, saying, "If I were to hand over one million RMB, the technological improvements currently underway would have to stop, the improvements in housing and benefits for our employees would be put on hold, and some funds would have to be retrieved from workers who were paid bonuses on the basis of their performance. What's more, we would have no possibility of paying workers this month." He implied that payment would require coercion. One month later, Deng Xiaoping issued a notice saying that all Capital Steel's contractual terms would stay the same.

The Capital Steel episode was in fact a contest between two different interest groups within one State-owned asset group. The same conflict has been played out between virtually all State-owned enterprises and their administrative overseers since that time. People quickly discovered that although the *cheng-bao* system worked to the extent that productivity went up, there was no clear demarcation of ownership and the benefits of ownership and therefore no way to resolve conflicts with administrative superiors. The flip side of this issue of not declaring ownership was that an enterprise could spend money at will and not be held accountable. Investments made by many State-owned enterprises surged upwards, with part of the money going into "business outside the Plan." Expenditures were uncontrollable since no-one was forced to take responsibility for the consequences of investments. Profits could be pocketed, but losses were someone else's problem. The idea was, "First make the cake bigger, we'll figure out how to divide it later." As to who was going to pay the bills, that was the State's problem.

In order to begin to get a handle on the situation, the Central Government decided to undertake taxation-system reform. The first major initiative in taking State-owned enterprises in the direction of becoming modern companies with corporate governance systems was therefore called "Changing profits to taxes." This was meant to release enterprises from the paternalistic system of "one big pot," even if the so-called release was a very small beginning and even though "Daddy" still took the lion's share of earnings. Looked at in hindsight and with an objective eye, the "profits to taxes" reform helped to ameliorate conflicts between enterprises and their administrators to a degree, and it also further motivated enterprises to perform. Inherent problems in the overall system were not addressed, however, tax categories were too uniform and the tax code was too blunt to use as a macro-economic tool in moderating the economy. Allocation of after-tax profits continued to be extremely complex, with a great deal of latitude for certain interest groups. Even more importantly, the reform did not address the problem of what should happen when an enterprise ran into trouble and had serious losses. It did not set any parameters on who was to bear responsibility. State-owned enterprises still ate from the same big pot; the profit-to-tax reform merely addressed part of the limited issue of who got how much from that pot.

As a part of the debate surrounding reform of State-owned enterprises, the theory of the "bird-in-a-cage economy" now began to circulate. The general thinking behind this was that any given enterprise was like a bird and you couldn't keep it alive if you tied down its wings. At the same time, the overall economic system of China was like a large birdcage in which these birds should be allowed to fly. They should not, however, be allowed to escape from the confines of the birdcage. In the end, this way of thinking got the upper hand in policy circles and the birdcage theory ruled over enterprise-reform throughout the remainder of the 1980s. Debate about reform itself became a kind of "reform within a cage."

The halting nature of State-owned enterprise reform was to continue for the next twenty years. Not until around the year 1998 was anyone willing to grapple with the hyper-sensitive issue of ownership. As a result, State-owned enterprises remained moribund, which paradoxically and fortuitously provided room for a very vital grass-roots movement of private enterprise to grow.

Nian Guangjiu and his 'Sha-zi Gua-zi' stall.

Shooting Stars in the Countryside

In 1979, an incident in a place called Wuhu in Anhui Province gave China's theoreticians a very tricky problem to resolve. It was initiated by a man named *Sha-zi*, which in Chinese means the Fool.

The Fool made his living by stir-frying melon seeds, which in Chinese is pronounced *gua-zi*. The case of the Fool's melon seeds was to plague policy-makers for years to come. Since his melon seeds were delicious and the name of his foodstall, *Sha-zi Gua-zi,* was so appealing, the Fool was soon employing twelve workers. According to proper Marxism as described in *Das Kapital,* if an employer hires more than eight people he can no longer be considered small enterprise but instead should be thought of as someone who is exploiting the masses. He should be considered a capitalist. The question came to the attention of authorities: was the Fool exploiting the masses or not?

GLOSSARY

Ge-ti-hu

Refers to a form of economic activity that was prevalent in recent Chinese history but is fast disappearing. The words are the abbreviation of a longer term that means "individual industrial and commercial household or entity." *Ge-ti-hu* included three different forms, those managed by an individual, by a household, and by a partnership. *Ge-ti-hu*s were permitted to operate under State laws within a certain policy-permitted scope of operations. They were allowed to carry on business in industry, handicrafts, services, repair businesses as well as other trades. "Individual" indicates that a person was generally self-employed, and he owned his business, as opposed to the State owning the business. Since *ge-ti-hu* took on liability themselves and were not legal entities, they were different from a limited liability form of entity in China called "privately managed enterprise."

The first group of 'individual small-time entrepreneurs' on the streets of Shanghai in July 1980. This photograph was allowed to be taken but not to be published due to regulations that allowed certain things to be shown in the media 'only to an appropriate degree.' The photo was stashed away in the drawer of the photo-journalist.

Should he be considered a capitalist and dealt with accordingly? An extremely ideological debate ensued. It continued all the way up to 1982, by which time the Fool's factory was employing 105 people, producing 9,000 kilos of melon seeds per day, and making a sum of money that was said to exceed RMB 1 million. As for how many people a small-time operator could hire without being considered exploitative, the debate simply raged on. In the end, it was Deng Xiaoping who brought the question to closure with typical political finesse. In front of the Politburo of the Central Committee of the Communist Party, he declared that, with respect to judging privately-managed enterprises, the government should adopt a posture of "wait and see."

It is unthinkable in the context of today's reality for a small-time vendor to stir up such a huge controversy. In the early days of reform and opening up, however, many people looked on any privately-operated business

The technology for making hand-made woks was almost lost, when small-time free enterprise resumed in the Zhabei District in Shanghai. This photo shows a father teaching his son the trade. They were able to make nearly RMB 200 per month in 1980.

Deng Xiaoping in a meeting with former Prime Minister of the U.K., Margaret Thatcher.

as the very incarnation of a "capitalist tail."

In point of fact, while this debate about the Fool's melon seeds was going on China's interior, the hyper-dry kindling of a privately-operated economy was igniting along in the coast in such places as Guangdong, Fujian, and Zhejiang.

In the region of Wenzhou in Zhejiang Province, a continuous stream of smugglers was guiding fishing boats piled with consumer goods into tiny ports along the coast. Local officials adopted an attitude of "one eye open, one shut" towards this importing of clothes, electronics, and hardware, since they and their small communities benefited by the trade. As a result, small market centers began to spring up as an important source of goods for sale on into China's interior. Buyers were those small peddlers brave and tough enough to take on product and sell it as itinerant peddlers in the countryside. Mainly, this meant people from the region of Wenzhou. These savvy traders formed the very first contingent of private businessmen in China. By 1980, there were more than 3,000 *ge-ti-hu* or small-time private businessmen doing trade on their own account. The business was most active in places where townspeople from different villages converged, and small workshops began to appear in these business nodes as well. They generally specialized in a specific product. By 1983, more than

The victorious Chinese women's volleyball team in the 1980s.

100,000 such home-based small industries operated in Wenzhou, employing some 400,000 people. In most years, a sales force of 100,000 Wenzhou peddlers would spread out over the entire country, selling goods and purchasing raw materials. Later, people described the hardships these people endured as the "spirit of those who have been through the four 'thousands.'" This referred to enduring a thousand hardships, giving a thousand spiels, traveling a thousand hard miles, and dreaming up a thousand schemes and tricks to get people to buy their wares. Today, you can find Wenzhou people doing business in every part of the world. Their organizational network, based on blood ties and allegiance to their local turf, is global and highly effective.

It is worth pointing out that people who engaged in small private enterprises in the early days came, almost exclusively, from the lowest levels of Chinese society. Frequently they were unemployed, people who had committed crimes, and people with a low level of education and literacy. Young intellectual people, or "*zhi-qing*," who were returning to cities

GLOSSARY

Zhi-qing

Or "intellectual youth." The Chinese term is an abbreviation referring to young people with a certain degree of education and specifically to a unique group of people who experienced a particular chapter in China's history. Around sixteen million young people were sent from urban homes to farming villages in the 1960s and 1970s, to join either collective "troops" or government-operated farms. Most had a primary school or middle school education.

 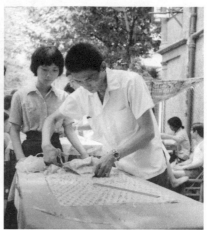

after being "sent down to the countryside," were an exception to a degree, but all these various groups including the last had been excluded from the "warmth" of the system. They were forced to take a different route in order to survive, and the route they took meant there was no turning back. Many among these people had highly acute entrepreneurial instincts. Their adaptability was astonishing. One tiny ray of light, coming through some crack, would be enough to allow them to grow upwards like a rocket.

Left: A *ge-ti-hu* owned by a couple was receiving good business.

Right: A tailor stand on the street.

In contrast to these private enterprises, growing amid cracks, the concurrent development of what were called "township-and-village enterprises" was quite dramatic.

After the start of reform and opening up, the government began to encourage the development of commune-based enterprises as a way to ameliorate economic hardship in farming villages. These were given strict guidelines by the government. They were to adhere firmly to the "direction of socialism," they were primarily to serve the needs of agricultural production and to make useful and necessary products, and they were to provide goods needed in larger-scale industries and for export. They were absolutely forbidden to make products in which there was a surplus of productive capacity, they were forbidden also to "cook a meal without rice," which in the Chinese

OUTFOXING YELTSIN
Gorbachev Fights Off a Challenge

Newsweek
THE INTERNATIONAL NEWSMAGAZINE

Making China Work

Against All Odds, Capitalism Is Taking Hold

Factory manager
Lu Guanqiu

Lu Guanqiu was the first Chinese entrepreneur to be on the cover of *Newsweek* magazine.

context means to make bricks without straw, or to make substandard products. They were not to compete for raw materials with larger-scale industrial enterprises, and they were not to damage State resources in any way. China's peasants have never lacked for intelligence, however. Among them, many are deeply patriotic but also highly attuned to opportunity, especially since most of them have been faced with the need to survive. China's farmers were willing to do whatever survival required. At an early date, many began to supplement their farming activities with other forms of business.

A few examples should suffice. In Xiaoshan in Zhejiang Province, a local farmer, born and bred, could be seen riding an old bicycle up and down alleys collecting any scrap metal he could find. With it, he made whatever people might need. When word got out and people learned about him, they were amazed to find that he had been quietly doing this already for ten years. In the fall of 1978, this man, named Lu Guanqiu, began to specialize in making those automobile spare parts that wear out most quickly. In order to force his way into the market, he began to set up a little booth outside trade fairs that admitted only State-owned enterprises. He set his prices 20% lower than any prices on the inside. In 1993, the enterprise that Lu Guanqiu founded became the first township-and-village enterprise to be listed on the stock exchange.

In Jiangyin County, Jiangsu Province, another man was quietly doing business even as the debate about "tails of capitalism" raged around him. This was Wu Renbao, Party Secretary of Huaxi Village. Wu Renbao secretly set up a little workshop in the fields, making hardware items. When officials came by, everyone would be seen working in the fields. When they left, farmers would go back to their benches and make hardware. Wu Renbao was able single-handedly to create a highly lucrative industrial kingdom. In 1999, his village became the first place as a village to raise money on the capital markets.

In the mid-1980s, the spirit of a market economy quietly touched down here and there upon the countryside in China. While reform and opening up was still being debated, the wheel of history was gathering momentum and could not be reversed. People were aware that the world had changed and their energies now began to burst out in all directions. By the time Deng Xiaoping declared, "Let some of the people get rich first," getting rich was already the common goal of most Chinese. A materialistic era was soon to roll across the country.

PART TWO

Commotion and Tumult
1984–1992

1

1. The Chinese team reappears at the 23rd Asian Games in 1984.

2. The Chinese marksman Xu Haifeng takes a gold medal at the Asian Games, July 29, 1984.

3. As the parade passed through Tian'anmen Square, students from Peking University pulled out a banner reading, 'Hello, Xiaoping!', which expressed the positive sentiment of the common man towards him.

4. Deyang County in Sichuan in 1984: farmers coming in to the big city.

5. Parade celebrating National Day, October 1, 1984. The message on the slogans is different this year and relates to the new 'cheng-bao' system.

6. The first group of people to get motorcycle licenses in 1984.

7. People purchasing the Chinese cabbge for the whole winter in 1984.

1984, the "Founding Year" of Major Chinese Enterprises

2

1984 was a year of suggestive overtones. George Orwell's novel had predicted a totalitarian era. Not only did this not come to pass in capitalist countries, but in China a different scenario was being played out with abandon as private enterprise swept through the country. Instead of the normal greeting in the morning, "Have you eaten?" people would say to each other, "Have you jumped into the ocean yet?" This meant, "Have you taken the big step and left the security of a State-funded unit to start in private enterprise on your own." Other sayings were going around, about how it was more lucrative to wield a barber's knife than a surgeon's, to sell eggs rather than work on guided missiles. The three most desirable jobs

3

4

5

6

7

in 1984, according to a survey done by the *China Youth Daily*, were taxi driver, private trader, and chef. The three worst jobs were scientist, doctor, and teacher.

It was an emotional and thrilling time. Chinese people had been through some crazy times, but they now appeared to be moving into one of the craziest in their lives.

In January of 1984, Deng Xiaoping traveled south to Guangdong Province, which was already in the midst of springtime. Not long before his trip, a newspaper in the north had published an article that was titled "Concessions Make a Comeback." This was aimed at the new "concession" of Shenzhen, and compared Shenzhen to imperial China's practice of leasing out its land to foreigners in Hong Kong and elsewhere. Other articles warned that China had to guard against a reappearance of "compradores," those people who sold out the country by serving as intermediaries for Western businesses. China had to guard against the reappearance of people like Li Hongzhang, the Viceroy who conducted China's foreign policy in the late Qing Dynasty and was felt by some to have paid too high a price for relations with the West. Many old cadres who came to look over Shenzhen were horrified by what it represented. "Other than the five-star Chinese flag, you can't find a single bit of socialism in this place." They demanded an answer to the rhetorical question, "Is this Special Economic Zone socialist? Or is it not really capitalist?!" Deng Xiaoping went south to view the region in person and to figure out what should be done and how to respond to the attacks. He did not say a word on the way down, and he gave no indication of his thinking.

After visiting Shenzhen, Deng Xiaoping went to the nearby Special Economic Zone called Zhuhai. Here he abandoned his

> ## GLOSSARY
>
> ### Zu-jie
>
> Or "concession." After the 1840 Opium War, various powers forced Qing China's government to demarcate special areas in ports along the coast or in major cities where their citizens could work and live. Japanese and European governments achieved these "concessions" through the use of unequal treaties. Two types of concession were formed, one governed by a single power, and another by a group of powers. Municipal governing structures were set up in the concessions that had both administrative and judicial powers. China generally did not dare interfere. The concessions were seen in China as a visible symbol of the loss of sovereign power. Concessions within China did not end until 1945, when the War of Resistance against Japan was won by China.

silent approach and wrote a commemorative message with a few brief words of praise, "The Zhuhai Special Economic Zone is excellent." This appeared to be the final word on the subject. On February 1, already back in Guangzhou, Deng Xiaoping finally wrote another commemorative couplet at the urging of leaders of Guangdong Province and of Shenzhen City. He wrote, "The growth and experience of Shenzhen prove that we were correct in our policy of setting up Special Economic Zones." He sealed this official approval by putting the date as January 26, 1984, meaning he had already decided to support the Zones when he was in Shenzhen. With Deng Xiaoping's decisive approval, a debate that had been raging on the merits of Special Economic Zones since 1981 was put to rest.

In concert with this southern initiative, the first generation of China's entrepreneurs set out on the road to success in 1984. Their activities followed a shift in the focus of reform policies from farming villages to cities, which allowed the birth of a number of companies. The year 1984 was later to be recognized as the Founding Year of many of China's major modern enterprises.

China's early entrepreneurs were destined to follow a circuitous path, but in the end the most important among them survived and prospered. In Qingdao City in Shandong Province, thirty-five-year-old Zhang Ruimin was sent by the authorities to take charge of a electronics factory that was on the verge of collapse. He later recalled, "Greeting me on my first day in the factory were 53 requests from employees to be transferred to some other place. Work started at 8 o'clock in the morning but people would start leaving by 9 and by 10 o'clock you could have thrown a hand grenade into the factory yard and not hurt anyone. Inside the factory yard, the ground was so dirty that after a rain you had to hold ropes under your feet as you walked along. Otherwise your boots would have been sucked off in the mud." The first thing Zhang Ruimin did to restore discipline was post notices on the walls, "Forbidden to urinate or defecate inside the factory." One time, he personally destroyed 76 sub-standard refrigerators, to the dismay of employees. Ten years later, the Haier Group that he founded

had become China's largest manufacturer of home electronics. Not only had it won a top place in the domestic market, but it had been able to break into international markets as well.

In the northern district of Zhongguancun in Beijing, an engineer named Liu Chuanzhi went to work everyday in 1984 at the very prestigious Computer Research Institute. He had nothing at all to do there, however, and out of sheer frustration he finally founded a company, securing permission to make its headquarters the tiny guard's room at the entryway to the compound. With great confidence, he said to his superiors, "In the future, our company is going to be so big it will be doing RMB 2 million of business per year." That sum was equal to around one million US dollars at the time, while the annual turnover of Lenovo is in the billions today. When he first started, Liu Chuanzhi ran around like a headless ant, bicycling up and down alleys to get things done. He set up a little stand outside the front gate and tried to sell watches and sandals. Later he did a wholesale business in gym pants and refrigerators. He himself had no idea that the company he founded would lead the IT industry one day, and become one of China's reigning brands. He could not have imagined that Lenovo would be purchasing IBM's PC business and going into global competition against the world's giants.

1. 1984: Zhang Ruimin of the Haier Company used a hammer to smash substandard refrigerators. In an age of scarcity, substandard goods were allowed to be sold. 'Smashing the refrigerators' started awareness of quality control among Chinese enterprises.

2. On November 1, 1984, with RMB 200,000, eleven scientists 'jumped into the ocean' and founded an enterprise that was later to become Legend and still later become, Lenovo. The office was located in an abandoned guard's room at the gate of the Academy of Science.

3. Wang Shi, speaking at the founding of the Shenzhen Modern Scientific Instruments Exhibition Center. This company later changed its name to Vanke. In 2008, it was the largest real estate company in China.

The founding ceremony of Wolkswagon in Shanghai, October 1984.

In hot Shenzhen in the south, a young man named Wang Shi spent all his days in 1984 buying and reselling corn. From this business, he progressed to founding a trading company. The secret to his success was his ability to obtain foreign exchange quota as allocated to the Special Economic Zone by advantageous government policies. He used the foreign exchange to import products into the Zone during a period when there was a ferocious appetite in China for goods and only one channel through which those goods could be imported. He quickly made enough money to serve as "initial capital" for the company that he founded, called Vanke. Vanke has since become the largest urban real estate developer in China and Wang Shi is now one of China's most successful and most respected real estate developers.

In the Pearl River Delta, the factory manager of a small county-level alcoholic beverages factory went to Guangzhou one day and saw that people were drinking something called Coca-Cola. Li Jingwei returned to his factory with the idea of producing non-alcoholic beverages as well. A member of the Athletic Commission, he heard that someone had developed a miracle drink that allowed athletes to achieve better performance. Not long after, Li Jingwei began making a similar kind of "oriental spirit water" named *Jian-li-bao*, a name that implies

Cars, bicycles, and horse-drawn carts shared the road in the outskirts of Beijing in 1984. This scene was to continue until the mid-1990s.

a fortifying health drink. For the next fifteen years, Jianlibao was regarded as the number one brand in beverages in China.

Also in around 1984, a professor in the Army Medical Institute named Zhao Xinxian began a new business near Brushrest Hills, in Shenzhen. This was to become the 999 Group, the most famous pharmaceutical enterprise in China. In Huizhou, Guangdong Province, Li Dongsheng, a young man who had graduated from the South China University of Technology started his factory in a dilapidated warehouse that housed old tractors and agricultural equipment. He cooperated with some Hong Kong people in producing the tape used in tape-recording. The illustrious home electronics company called TCL grew out of this humble beginning.

In a small town in the country of Shunde in Guangdong Province, a man named Pan Ning, with no more than a fourth-grade education, fashioned the prototype for China's first two-door refrigerator out of primitive tools. He made the model out of old soda-pop cans, hammered and drilled into something that actually worked. Rain was pelting down on the day that his model ran successfully—when he saw this, he charged out into the torrent, weeping for joy.

The period was worthy of pride on the part of many entrepreneurs, yet it was also one that many entrepreneurs

Upper left: Winter 1985, a collective market, a group of stolid farmers has fun at a game of pool. In the early 1980s, pool, formerly held to be an 'aristocrats' game,' became popular throughout China with astonishing speed.

Upper right: Summer 1985, next to Chaoyang Lake in Pujiang County, Sichuan. Young people dancing to the tune of a popular singer, Teresa Teng

Lower: Factory heads in Fuzhou, after they have publicized their request for 'loosening the bonds that tie us.' This provoked a positive reaction throughout the country, and the day of the 'release us' announcement became 'Factory Manager Day' in the country.

do not want to remember. In the course of setting up their companies, essentially all of these men involved themselves in "grey-market" areas as they built up initial capital. Their family backgrounds were different, their characters were different, but the one thing they shared was passion and determination. Each one fully intended to break out into a new world. Although many had just begun to learn the ABCs of a market economy, their energy and spirit in founding companies and their survival instincts were superlative. They made full use of the Chinese concept of "eight sages traveling the oceans, their senses attuned to and connecting with all around them," even as they underwent a baptism of mar-

ketizing forces in China and globalizing forces around the world.

While this first generation of entrepreneurs was founding companies, China's State-owned enterprises remained "inside the cage" of the planned-economy system. They remained an ongoing headache to the government.

On March 24, 1984, a group of fifty-five factory heads of State-owned enterprises in backbone industries in Fujian Province sent out a cry for help. This cry for help was titled, "Please loosen the bonds on us," and its entire text was published in the *Fujian Daily*, which was an unheard of breach of discipline. The article stated that under the current system, the managers were tied hand and foot, the enterprises were facing suffocating pressures, no motivation, no vitality. The specific ways in which they asked that the bonds be loosened included the following. First, with regard to more autonomy in employment decisions, they asked that they be given full right to hire and to fire, with the exception of appointment of the factory chief who should be appointed by superiors. They asked for permission for the factory chief to appoint his deputy, with review of qualifications and approval by authorities. Second, with regard to the right to decide on budgeting and finance, they wanted authority to decide upon and distribute bonuses, without outside interference. Third, with regard to managing the business of the company, after the quota for State-mandated production had been fulfilled, as under the Plan, they asked to be allowed to arrange for and utilize inputs for further production on their own account. They asked to be able to sell the production at prices that were allowed the latitude of "high-in high-out" and "low-in low-out." The local government immediately issued a response that was in full support of the requests. It said, "We will not be a new mother-in-law, we resolutely support reform, we support the loosening of bonds and the transfer of authority on down the line." One week later, the *People's Daily* in Beijing placed a positive report on these fifty-five factory chiefs in a prominent position. The news that managers had called for a loosening of the bonds was accompanied by editorials supporting their requests. Relevant authorities at the provincial level in Fujian were encouraged to respond favorably to the call.

For the first time, this "open letter" raised the subject of implementing a "factory head's (manager's) Responsibility System," which was meant to stimulate active response from managers by transferring certain rights and responsibilities on down to their level. This quickly became common knowledge around the country. On May 10, the State Council issued "Provisional Regulations on further expanding the autonomy of State-operated industrial enterprises." Not long after, it put out "Various decisions on reform of urban economic systems." Within the next two years, the State Council issued a number of documents promoting a "Responsibility System for Factory Heads/Managers," clearly stipulating that the factory head (manager), in industrial enterprises owned by all the people, was the Head of the factory, that he was the Legal-person Representative of the enterprise, that he held all responsibility with regard to the enterprise, that he was in a central position and played a central role.

Throughout the Deng Xiaoping period, the government never stopped reforming State-owned enterprises for a single day, whether it was to pursue the *cheng-bao* system or the "Factory Head/Manager Responsibility System." However, since property ownership was unclear, relying solely on "internal reform" to raise efficiency was bound to fail in the end. Reforms to save State-owned companies or enterprises were effective for a while, but given later conditions could only have a transient effect. Fortunately, the stumbling and erratic progress of these reforms gave breathing room to newly established collective township-and-village enterprises and privately-operated enterprises.

GLOSSARY

Head of the factory (manager) responsibility system

The system whereby one person, the "Head of the factory," was in charge and was also the factory's legal-person representative. Before this system, each State-owned enterprise in China had two responsible people. One was the Secretary of the Communist Party Commission; the other was the Head of the Factory (Manager). The term "Manager" is put in parentheses because it was only gradually adopted as the proper term. The promotion of this new system rectified a situation in which responsibility between Party representatives and actual Managers was unclear.

A flood of bicycles at dawn in Shanghai, 1991.

A Two-track Pricing Policy and a Trip to Hainan Island

Events on Hainan Island in the 1980s seem like a long-ago fairytale by now. People find it hard to believe what took place there, except for those who actually participated in the events. News from Hainan, of "victory on the front," quickly wafted into the mainland of China and drew hundreds of thousands of profit-seekers to the island. These were part of that army of people who had "jumped into the ocean" by severing ties with their former "unit" and its security. All came with a single purpose. Many were able to make a tremendous amount of money and escape with it before policies changed. In the course of their business ventures, this little island became as sacred to them as the revolutionary "Yan'an." They approached its shores with emotions that verged on worship, and unwittingly were able to be part of an epochal period in China.

Two months after Deng Xiaoping made his trip to Guangdong in early 1984, the Central Committee of the Communist Party of China made a historic decision. It announced "the opening of fourteen coastal

GLOSSARY

Yan'an

A city located in the northern part of Shaanxi Province where the central organizations of the Communist Party of China were located from 1937 to 1948.

cities to foreign investment as well as the opening of Hainan Island." Hainan was a solitary piece of paradise in the middle of the south seas. The island covers an area of 35,000 square kilometers. Before reform and opening up, it had essentially no industry due to the island's strategic military importance. It was simply beautiful fields and beaches, a place inhabited by very simple people. This suddenly changed in the mid-1980s when fate came knocking violently at Hainan's door and the island was thrust onto the frontlines of reform.

Fate may have come too suddenly. Local governments had no time for adequate "thought preparation." Local policy makers did remember the classic quotation about borrowing arrows from the enemy by sending out straw boats. They figured out how to turn the "Special-policy status" of Hainan into pure gold. According to a document issued by the State Council, "the Hainan Administrative Region is authorized to import production materials for industry and agriculture as conditions require, which are to be used in production and construction. The Region may utilize its local reserves of foreign exchange in order to import consumer goods that are in short supply in Hainan markets (including those import items that are controlled by the State)." Good at calculations, Hainan people quickly discovered that this was a shortcut to wealth. In an instant, a tidal wave of "business dealing for one's own personal gain" swept over the place. In Chinese, the term is "*zou-si*" or engaging in private-interest deals, including smuggling.

Once the gates were open, the situation could not be retrieved. The Hainan of 1984 was still a place where both officials and people were extremely poor. The entire government budget of the island was RMB 285.6 million. In the words of a local official, "We didn't even have enough for salaries. And

GLOSSARY

**Borrowing arrows
by using straw boats**

This proverb is known to all in China. During the Three Kingdoms period (3rd century AD), the combined forces of Sun Quan and Liu Bei engaged in a huge battle with Cao Cao at the Red Cliffs. The two settled down on opposite sides of the Yangtze River, at the narrows. Before the battle, Zhuge Liang, who was Liu Bei's primary strategist, sent twenty small boats packed full of straw off in the heavy mist towards the other side of the river. Not being able to see what he was up to, Cao Cao's armies shot the boats absolutely full of arrows, at which the boats were retrieved to the other shore. More than 100,000 arrows were obtained in this way, according to the legend. Zhuge Liang used this ingenious trickery to obtain a wealth of ammunition from his own enemy and the underlying concept has been used to this day.

1. 1983, a fashionable young lady is getting her ears pierced.
2. Cosmetics.
3. Lively market scene.
4. Street scene in a small city.
5. A stream of 'peasant labor' heads out to find jobs. Photograhed in 1985 at Liping, Guizhou.
6. Agricultural workers or 'peasant workers' in the mid-1980s, who had left the farms to find work in the city.

when local towns were supposed to hang out signs saying the 'communes' had been changed to 'townships,' they didn't have enough money for the signs. When it was time to recruit soldiers into the army, there was no money for the paper for the recruiting banners. That is the truth." Now, all anyone had to do was to get hold of an import authorization and he could make instant money. By reselling a document allowing one to import a car, for example, one could make RMB 10,000. So far as people on Hainan were concerned, this was just like having an oil well open up by your front door. The island was soon immersed in a frenzy of trying to get hold of import authorizations. Everyone was wanting to *"dao-mai"* cars, or buy and resell the paper for importing them, at a profit. Senior government officials were later to admit, ruefully, "Even kindergartens were dealing in authorizations to import cars. Those authorizations could be turned into money. You'd take them to other provinces and sell them. They didn't have authorizations. Hainan did! Just by turning a piece of paper around, selling it to someone else, you'd make money!"

In the summer of 1984, practically everyone on Hainan was talking "cars." You would hear the conversations in teahouses, restaurants, hotels, shops, government organizations, factories, schools, newspapers, yes even in kindergartens and day-care centers. In a place where they had not existed before, everyone had expanded his vocabulary to include this term: cars. In the first half of 1984, Hainan imported just 2,000 cars. But in July, the local government suddenly authorized the import of

Left: Shanghai in 1986. The bicycle brand called 'Forever' was popular at the time.

Right: A Shanghai street scene in 1986. Back then, it was an extremely wonderful thing to be able to take home electronics back to one's home.

13,000 cars, 36 times the monthly average of the first half of the year. The black market for foreign currency became an openly traded market, and the price of foreign exchange rose wildly. One US dollar to one RMB went to 1 to 4.4 from 1 to 1.5 before July 1984, and even 1 to 6. People brought in huge bundles of RMB and surged toward the Pearl River Delta area to turn it into Hong Kong dollars. Many in Shenzhen, Beijing and other places were similarly quick to smell the scent of gold in this Hainan policy. At the time, the import of home electronics and other consumables was severely restricted in China. One had to get permission directly from the State Council. Cars, motorcycles, spare parts, all were restricted. Hainan Island now had its own special right to import, and any fool could judge the profit margins in this situation. Hainan became irresistible.

Within six months, the Hainan Fever was over. Only a few "rotten-tail buildings" stood around in the rain to indicate the glorious days that had just passed. Due to the unequal pace of economic development in various regions of China, during the early periods of reform and opening up this phenomenon was bound to happen. The moment the floodgates opened, all resources and energy would flow into

Left: An old man doing small-scale business in 1987. He was able to make a few RMB per day.

Right: In 1986, a group of State-managed shops were openly sold at auction in Beijing and changed to private ownership.

GLOSSARY

Lan-wei-lou

Or rotten-tail buildings, refers to real estate projects that have been put on hold or abandoned for one year or more, due to inability of the developers to continue the investment, to legal disputes about debts, or sometimes because the engineering does not come up to adequate standards. Any of these issues could lead to rotten-tail buildings.

Left: Massive fires occurred at Great Hinggan Range in 1987, which first alerted people to the importance of environmental protection.

Right: Hula hoops were the rage in 1989.

low-lying ground, to soak up any possible profits. The situation led to unthinkable unintended consequences. In Hainan as well as elsewhere, policy makers then had to address the problems with multiple remedial measures.

Stimulated by the Hainan Fever, in the mid-1980s all of China was in an economic fever as well. Credit increased ferociously, the Central Bank printed money night and day, and the entire country was swamped in a wave of imported foreign equipment.

From 1985 to 1987, China imported 115 color television production lines, 73 refrigerator production lines, 15 copier production lines, 35 aluminum-material fabricating production lines, 22 integrated circuit production lines, and 6 frosted-glass production lines, among other things. The one province of Guangdong alone imported 21 textile production lines, 18 beverage containerization production lines, 22 food packaging production lines, 12 furniture production lines. *Newsweek* published an article which described the situation in vivid terms. "A group of engineers, technical people, and packaging workers arrived at an industrial town in France and began to work day and night dismantling and packaging a refrigerator factory that had gone bankrupt. They packed 5,000 tons of equipment into boats, planes, and trains, and shipped them off to

Tianjin. In Tianjin, a factory took the lot over and reconstructed it into a production line producing 2,000 new refrigerators every single day. The same kind of thing can be seen everywhere in China. Throughout Europe, Chinese delegations can be seen with their hands clutching lists of things they want to buy, looking for second-hand factories and equipment. To European companies this is a great blessing. If they did not sell the equipment, they would destroy it or let it sit idle. China is also an extremely seductive trading partner, because China always pays in cash." By the end of 1985, China's negative trade balance stood at a record USD 13.78 billion, about equal to 52% of its exports.

Due to the economic overheating, enterprises soon were facing shortages of raw materials. In order to protect the interests of State-owned enterprises, the government finally settled on a policy of a "two-track pricing system." This decision was to lead the Chinese economy into a cataclysmic upheaval.

What this two-track pricing system meant was that for any given raw material used in production there would be two prices. One was the "inside-the-Plan price," controlled by the State, and intended for State-owned enterprises. The other was the market-driven "outside-the-Plan price," intended for privately-operated enterprises and collective enterprises. The inherent costs of the outside-the-Plan price were far higher than the inside-the-Plan price.

The unintended consequences of this policy soon escaped the bounds of policy-makers expectations. The two-price system for raw materials immediately evolved into a crazy game. "Resellers," traders who could see opportunity a thousand miles away, instantly began an arbitrage business in the margin between the two prices. From one hand to the next, it was buy and sell, buy and sell. A ton of steel might go through several hands in reaching a final buyer, and double in price as a result. Attracted by what in China are called "explosive profits," the prices of all kinds of government-mandated "allocated goods and materials" became, *de facto*, market-driven. Materials slipped out of allocated factories and units and, via all kinds of channels and through all kinds of hands, found their

On May 9, 1986, the rock'n'roll performer Cui Jian first sang *Without Anything* and brought down the house. This was the cover of one of Cui Jian's best-selling tapes.

natural price level among a regular market. The command economy of the government totally lost any rigor or control. In fact, in the years in which China implemented a two-track pricing system, State-allocated goods and materials were not able to complete a single contract for supply to the State. Any State-operated enterprise that honorably abided by the State Plan became immediate road kill. State-operated enterprises did not benefit from this policy. Resellers profited most, and they included all kinds of government officials. It can be said that the actions of these officials were the last straw in leading to the collapse of China's planned economy.

According to one report put out by people studying the issue, in the year 1988 alone, the total margin between State-controlled

Poetry was the primary medium through which the idealism of the 1980s was expressed. The modern poetry exhibition of 1986 was a major event.

goods and market prices exceeded RMB 150 billion. Add to that the difference in preferential and nonpreferential interest rates on bank loans and the exchange rate differential between the controlled rate and the market quotation, and the sum comes to over RMB 350 billion, or roughly 30% of 1988's national income. Of this amount, 70% is believed to have flowed into private pockets.

Faced with these unintended consequences, one economist who espoused the two-track pricing system at the time, said, with a bitter laugh, "We sowed dragon seeds. But what we reaped were fleas."

As for how history will evaluate the two-track pricing system, there has been and continues to be debate among economists. Some feel that the two-track pricing system allowed opportunism to become entrenched and systemic, creating large-scale corruption. Others feel that this way of doing things was a success, and they frame their reasoning in the form of a counter-question. If China had not implemented a two-track pricing system, the country had only two choices. It could either continue along the planned-economy single track, or use shock therapy to enter a single-track market system. The former was not a viable solution; that was already an undisputed fact. The latter, these people feel, would not only have led to widespread disorder but would have brought on all kinds of other problems. Once markets were "opened" to market-driven forces, the original economic structures would not immediately have changed, for monopolistic State-owned enterprises would have used their special interests and special privileges to raise their prices. Before normal economic links

Left: At the first Great Wall Cup bodybuilding competition in May 1987, female contestants went on stage in bikini suits for the first time in Beijing.

Right: April 1988, at the first bodybuilding competition held in Yunnan Province, with curious onlookers standing outside the stadium.

The first group of people from Taiwan to come 'back home' arrives in Beijing on January 21, 1988. On top of the Great Wall, they shouted, 'We're home!' This first delegation was mostly composed of old retired veterans from the KMT; returning had been a cherished dream for forty years.

were functioning smoothly, the economy would have experienced extreme volatility. The two-track pricing system maintained a planned price, a kind of anchor, while at the same time releasing a portion of the market to market-driven prices. Although this incubated corruption, these people feel that the system allowed non-State-owned institutions an opportunity to develop. It enabled them to enjoy fast growth under the unconventional rules of the game of a two-track system.

Looked at today, this debate about a two-track system reflects the complexities of China's economy. Any type of reform in the direction of a market economy is bound to require the paying of a certain price in a culture that has experienced several thousand years of agricultural civilization. Any government has to contend with the question of how to maintain stability while at the same time stimulating the development of enterprises, the fundamental organisms of a market economy. How to carry out ongoing market reforms in an orderly fashion is a balancing act, for as the economy and the economic system changes in China, different kinds of asset ownership and enterprise ownership co-exist. The mixing of these types of ownership for personal gain is unavoidable when the economy is booming and people can benefit by playing the system. Policies at any given time may stir up debate but the overall situation moves in the right direction. The fortunate thing, and the thing to remember, is that China has not and will not turn around and go back in the other direction.

One aspect of China's economic reforms that should pro-
voke concern, however, is the explosive appearance of psychological imbalances among the general populace. Everyone
is thinking exclusively about how to make money, and a
fundamental shift in values is underway. The *People's Daily*
published an article about three young journalists who wrote
a book called *Historical Direction of China's Reform*. In it, the
journalists caution, "Reform is a particularly complex form of
'social systems engineering.' One cannot draw up a seamless
plan in advance and then simply implement it, for the process
involves ongoing change. In the course of the ongoing adjustments, friction and conflict between different interests groups
is going to be unavoidable."

This is not an easy thing to hear at this particular time,
since most people are still immersed in a kind of prostra-
tion before or homage to reform. They have not yet become
fully conscious of the repercussions of reform, specifically the
changes it is inflicting on China's social system. They are not
thinking about an overturn in fundamental concepts and a
lasting segmentation of social status.

On December 27, 1988, a painting exhibition showing previously forbidden oil paintings was put on display in Beijing. An average of 15,000 people came to see the exhibition every day.

Allowing Prices to "Break through the Pass"

In 1988, China welcomed a distinguished American visitor, Milton Friedman (1912–2006). The first Nobel prizewinner in economics to visit China, he was warmly received by the country's Central leaders. Nobody expected that his recommendations resulting from this trip would lead to the first major wave of ideological debate since reform and opening up began.

The reason China's leaders received Friedman was profoundly related to what was happening in the international arena at the time. The entire world was in ferment in the latter part of the 1980s, as liberation movements swept through Eastern Europe. Gorbachev had mobilized powerful social reforms in the Soviet Union, which eventually led to the dissolution of that largest socialist entity on the globe. In 1988, the Austrian economist Friedrich von Hayek (1899–1992), also a Nobel prizewinner, published a book entitled *The Fatal Conceit*. In this, he held that striving for a highly planned economy was a kind of "fatal conceit" on the part of "rationalists" and he systematically laid out the limitations of a planned economy. In an introduction he wrote that the kind of order that comes about spontaneously under circumstances that are not pre-designed greatly exceeds any plan that humans intentionally try to achieve. This was known as the "principle of spontaneous self-organization," which described a self-organizing system of voluntary cooperation. Hayek's book provided timely theoretical ammunition to capitalist countries in the West. In China it was held in some circles to be a veritable treasure.

China in 1988 was immersed in yet another economic fever. Several years of driving the economic engine at high speed had put the economic cycle in a very sensitive and unstable range. Supply of inputs was increasingly tight as the number of enterprises multiplied and light industry charged forward. More serious, however, was that the negative consequences of the two-track pricing system that had been operating for four years were ever more apparent.

These negative consequences related to the way in which the system could be manipulated for private gain. An article in China's *Economic Daily* propounded a "theory of how officials who resell commodities are bringing calamity upon the country." It stated bluntly that "prices of raw materials are soaring, and while the State issues edicts against raising prices, the results are minimal. The primary cause of this situation is that the government and enterprises are not separate. Officials and businessmen cannot be distinguished." It was just at this moment that Milton Friedman came to China.

As the main representative of the Chicago School of Economics, Friedman was an advocate of "economic freedom" and "free markets." He was known internationally for his work on price theory and monetary theory. He had offered a "prescription" for China which ran true to his free-market stance. He recommended that the Chinese government release commodity prices, for he felt that the Chinese reforms were already in their final stage. A Hong Kong paper, the *Hong Kong Economic Journal*, quoted him as saying, "One should not confuse the release of prices with inflation. If you release prices, only a portion of products will rise in price. People

GLOSSARY

Guan-dao

Speculators connected to officialdom or officials themselves ("*guan*"), who re-bought and re-sold goods for a profit. China's economic reforms were still at an experimental stage in the mid-1980s, and a two-track pricing system allowed some officials and their relatives to take advantage of buying at the lower official price and selling at the higher market price. Officials were in the privileged position of having access to "planned-economy goods" at the lower price, so they traded off their position. The explosive profits that were made in this period brought an acute sense of unfairness among the people at large, and even "hatred" of such officials.

Getting in line.

will feel some pain in the first few days but quickly will discover that prices will not necessarily ratchet on up."

While he was visiting Sichuan, Milton Friedman and the
governor of that province engaged in an amusing conversation that was widely broadcast throughout China. Friedman
told the governor, "If you want to cut off the tail of a mouse,
you shouldn't do it slowly, one piece at a time. You must do
it all at once. A short pain is better than a prolonged pain." In
response, the governor asked for Friedman's advice. "Professor,
you do realize of course that our Chinese mice are somewhat
different. They have many tails, all quite intertwined with each
other. Which do you think we should cut off first?" Friedman
had no response to this and simply shrugged his shoulders.
The Hong Kong economist Steven N.S. Cheung soon published an article that noted, "In fact we do have an answer to
the governor's question though we didn't say it at the time.
Our answer is to cut all the tails promptly, at the same time.
That should do the trick."

Friedman quickly found soul-mates in China who, like
him, wanted to cut all tails once and for all. These advocates
included some senior central government officials. They were
well aware that China's abnormal price volatility was the result
of both the planned-economy system and the two-track pricing
policy. They felt that in order to shuck off the entanglements of

a bizarre system they must use very decisive measures, namely, allowing pricing to be determined by market forces as soon as possible. The recommendations of the great price guru, Friedman, provided theoretical backing for their views.

A random survey undertaken by the China Economic System Reform Research Institute supported the idea that the Chinese people would approve of this approach. It interviewed basic-level enterprises and employees and the results gave Central great confidence. They indicated that 75.3% of the people felt that "we want reform to be done properly, and we are willing to take a lower standard of living for a while in order to achieve that." With Friedman's blessing and with this tacit approval of the people, the government therefore decided to loosen controls, to eliminate the two-track pricing system. It decided to implement a policy that was called "allowing prices to break on through the pass."

A dramatic time in China began as a result. The curtain was drawn open on a "movement to allow prices to rise," a movement that set people's hearts pounding with apprehension. In March of 1988, the "release of prices" began in the industrialized city of Shanghai with the uncoupling of price controls on 280 different commodities. Most of these were daily necessities and small items. Prices immediately rose between 20% and 30%. In April 1988, the State Council began implementing a proposal that allowed non-staple food prices to rise while allocating appropriate subsidies to employees. On May 19, the Xinhua News Agency issued the statement, "China's price reform is a courageous act, we must take a certain risk, but Central has confidence that this will be done properly and come out all right..." The policy and its repercussions quickly rippled across the entire country. Starting in May, the prices of pork and other meats in major urban centers rose by an average of 70%, and the prices of small items rose swiftly on the heels of food prices.

The policy of allowing prices to "break through the pass" quickly got out of hand. Inflation followed. With expectations of rising prices, people began a frenzy of buying and the panic was nationwide. According to contemporary reports, "People started buying whatever they saw in front of them, as if in a daze. They bought durables, but they also bought consumer goods and even what had previously been unsaleable items. If a television screen showed any kind of image, they bought it. If a fan could rotate, they bought it. If a refrigerator had electricity, they bought it." At the time, China had more than two hundred fan-producing factories with a total output of 34 million fans. The country was already the world's leading producer of fans and for two years supply had exceeded demand. Warehouses were bursting. Yet in this buying frenzy, warehouses were soon emptied of fans. In Guizhou, Yunnan, and other outlying provinces, people got into fights in the street over buying woolen yarn. In short order, people began to say that they could not take it, the price increases were too great. Professors in some universities were selling wonton soup, bread, eggs, and popsicles on the street—they couldn't make ends meet by relying on salaries alone.

The State Price Control Bureau noted in its *Price Yearbook of China* that prices rose faster in 1988 than in any year since 1950, that inflation was intense. Prices rose by over 95% among the 383 commodity retail price indicators by which the State calculates commodity prices.

The buying frenzy brought on by inflation also created unprecedented shortages in raw-material inputs for production. In May, the supply of coal for electric power generation in Shanghai was down to two days. Hundreds of thousands of enterprises were living from breath to breath. The wave of buying reached its peak in Shanghai on August 28, when the municipal government had to take emergency measures. It began distributing food, salt, and fuel again on the basis of coupons. You were only allowed to buy a cooking pot if you brought your old one in for exchange, or if you had a marriage certificate and evidence of your Shanghai residential status. On September 26, *Business Week* published a report called "The Twisting and Turning Path of China's Reforms." "China's reforms are losing control," it noted. "Price reform was frozen last month in order to deal with the crisis. The sudden about-face in government policy has brought uncertainty to both

Chinese and foreign investors. China is at present implementing emergency controls, and an economist in the Australian
Embassy has said, 'We are witnessing a blanket movement to
restore consumer confidence.'"

In October 1988, the policy decision to release price controls
was declared a failure. It was later judged to have brought on
the greatest loss of economic control since reforms began in
1978. The Central Government initiated policies to address the
situation that were known as "macro-adjustments, and harnessing and rectifying." The phrase was to resonate through
the next few years. Panic buying and price inflation had characterized the episode, but the release of price controls had not
led to a wholesale collapse of the economy. It had a negative
influence on the macro-economy, but production still went on.
Perhaps the more serious consequence was a loss of people's
enthusiasm for reform. In addition, there was now a growing
hatred for those officials who "used their position to trade on
the two-track system." There was an increasing recognition
that some were growing rich while the common people had to
face hardship due to inflation. From this point onward, there
was a growing impression in China that reform was creating a
radically unequal society.

The Chinese socialist economy now entered yet another
uncertain period. "Letting prices charge through the pass" had
not simply been a setback for economic policies—social unrest
now continued to extend into the future. When people realized
that reform was not going to be the prescription that solved all
problems, a groundswell of opposition began, just waiting to
break out.

A modern arts exhibition that generated much disputes in 1989.

"Harnessing and Rectifying"

People opened their *People's Daily* on New Year's Day of 1989 to read the following message from the government. "We have come up against unprecedented and grave problems. The most outstanding of these is inflation in our everyday lives, but there are also some negative and corrupt phenomena in Party and government and in society at large. All of these are of great concern and alarm to the people."

The Chinese New Year holidays had just passed when a wave of millions of workers began coming into cities. This happened in February 1989, and it galvanized local governments into swift action. Once the central government's price policy failed, the government had no choice but to begin "harnessing and rectifying the situation." This included putting an immediate stop to construction projects in cities, which meant that some five million "peasant workers" were out of their jobs. These people had come in from farming villages to cities to work and they were now forced to return to their rural homes. The economies in towns and villages turned out to be worse than in cities, however. The workers had no alternative but to turn around and try to find jobs again in cities. After

Kentucky Fried Chicken had just been allowed to enter China in 1989. The photograph was taken at Qianmen in Beijing.

Chinese New Year, when people traditionally go home for the holiday, millions of workers from the larger-population provinces of Henan, Sichuan, Hubei, and others began to clog the railroads and bus stations, trying to get into cities. The crush of people on the move was tremendous. Large and medium-sized cities faced enormous law-enforcement problems. On March 9, the General Office of the State Council issued an "Emergency Notice," requiring "strict controls on workers blindly coming into cities."

With the situation at fever pitch, privately operated enterprises became the first target of the government's "harnessing and rectifying" actions. In May, an investigation of tax evasion of enterprises began in Jiangsu Province, where the private economy in China was most thriving. The investigation concluded that 80% of enterprises were evading taxes, and that tax evasion was "extreme." A national movement to rectify this problem began. According to the *History of the PRC Economy*, in the second half of 1989, the number of *ge-ti-hu* or privately

The first McDonalds on the mainland of China opened at Dongmen in Shenzhen. This photograph was taken in January 2008.

registered businesses decreased by 3 million. Privately-administered enterprises went from 200,000 down to 90,600. This halving of the number of private enterprises did not change until 1991.

The second step the government took was to "clean up and rectify" the "new enterprises" outside the State-operated system. The new enterprises were felt to be sucking materials away from State-operated enterprises and causing inflation. They were regarded as traitors who had brought on national calamity by causing a loss of control over the market. In this rectifying movement, the emphasis was placed on companies that produced things like home electronics and particularly refrigerators. The latter had grown faster than anyone else and were now at the very epicenter of the storm. Somehow, these companies had been able to get State-produced or imported raw materials for their production, even though this was strictly forbidden. It seems they had gone through all kinds of "channels." In the past three years, if a company was not on a list of approved units, it was not allowed to import so much as a compressor, a ton of steel, even test results. It was not allowed to place ads in any media. Yet somehow these enterprises not only were able to get raw materials but were also able to increase in numbers. Sixty-six refrigerator plants operated in Hangzhou, Zhejiang Province, alone, where people-operated enterprises had grown the fastest. Many of those "not on the list" were producing 100,000 refrigerators per year, while it was interesting to note that official State-owned enterprises "on the list" not only had no new production lines, but many had never even built roofs over their heads.

China's economic growth rate in 1989 fell to its lowest level since 1978. Sources of financing dried up, consumer spending fell, factories couldn't stay open. Township-and-village enterprises shut down, unemployment increased, money stopped circulating. Because of a sudden social upheaval, positive changes that had been building over twelve years of reform, including a spirit of growing and developing, suddenly came up against a wall.

The failure of releasing price controls, in addition to social

turbulence and economic stagnation, now forced Chinese
policy makers into a new way of thinking about models for
reform. Activist thinking gradually receded and gave way
to a more mainstream line of thinking that was in favor of
gradual change. In 1989, Deng Xiaoping said, "The thing that
outweighs all other considerations when it comes to China's
problems is the question of stability." This term "stability" was
soon to be seen more frequently in the media than any other
noun. In the next year's New Year's Editorial, the *People's
Daily* stated, "We must maintain stability. Even if we have to
develop at a slow steady pace for ten years, China will achieve
fundamental change in the end."

Contrary to the expectations of many Western scholars,
China did not col-
lapse. The country
transitioned from
an overheated
economy to stable
growth and "open-
ing" again became
the main topic of
how to develop
the country. The

On November 9, 1989, Deng
Xiaoping expressed appre-
ciation to members of the
Communist Party of China for
accepting his formal resigna-
tion. On far left, Wan Li, head
of the Standing Committee
of the National People's Congress; on the far right, Jiang
Zemin, General Secretary of
the Central Committee of the
Communist Party; and, second from the right, Li Peng,
Premier of the State Council.

In 1990, when the Eleventh
Asian Games was held in Beijing, China's poor economic
situation had not yet begun to
revive. This photograph shows
the opening ceremony and
the raising of the flag.

Asian Games of 1990 could be regarded as a starting point in the process. In February of 1990, Deng Xiaoping made a special trip to celebrate Chinese New Year in Shanghai. On this occasion, he announced the decision to develop Pudong, the area across the Huangpu (Whampoa) River from the city of Shanghai. On April 18, Premier Li Peng and the State Council announced that the Central Committee of the Communist Party and the State Council had agreed to speed up developing this area. They announced policies that would make Pudong into a New Area as well as policies on the Special Economic Zones. The commitment to Pudong allowed Shanghai to become the "dragon head" of Chinese economic growth. The long term effects of this policy were enormous. From 1990 to 2004, Pudong's GDP grew to RMB 179 billion from a trivial RMB 6 billion. With one-eighth of the population of Shanghai and one-tenth of its land area, Pudong generated one-quarter of Shanghai's GDP and its industrial output, one-half of its exports, and one-third of its foreign investment. Within fifteen years, Pudong created the equivalent of another Shanghai. The Pudong area has become China's reigning financial center, as well as home to its most dense concentration of multinational headquarters. By the 1990 Central Plan, Pudong's favored treatment was to extend for fifteen years. In 2005, the State Council extended and expanded Pudong's status as an "experimental site" and authorized ongoing comprehensive reforms.

Left: Wang Shuo, author of a book called *Riffraff*, and film director Feng Xiaogang.

Right: Rock'n'roll fans letting loose.

If Pudong was one of the wings that allowed Shanghai to take flight, then the other wing was the establishment of the Shanghai Stock Exchange. On December 19, 1990, the Shanghai

Stock Exchange was opened amidst a great flurry of activity. Zhu Rongji, the future Premier, made the opening remarks. The person responsible for the Exchange beat a gong to announce the start of trading and promptly fainted on the floor from all the excitement. Chinese had not played the game of "capital" for forty years and there was a great deal of work to do to get things in order. Shenzhen, in the south, was facing similar challenges in the rush to get established. On December 1, just prior to Shanghai's opening, the Shenzhen Stock Exchange opened an "experimental market," in order not to be second to Shanghai. Due to the haste with which this was put together, the Shenzhen Exchange had no computerized systems like Shanghai. Only 8,000 shares were traded on the first day, using the most primitive method of calling out numbers and writing them up on a blackboard.

People were beginning to recover confidence, some sense that things were moving in a calm direction. China was gradually pulling out of an economic slump but anxieties about volatility remained. On top of these was concern about the evolving relationship between the Soviet Union and Eastern Europe, where the political situation was said to be worsening. Partially as a result of political developments overseas, another ideological debate began to percolate which suddenly

Left: The Shanghai Stock Exchange was established in 1990.

Right: In the early 1990s, the Wanguo Securities Company was one of the birthplaces of the Shanghai Stock Exchange. It was located at the corner of Xizang Road and Guangdong Road, in the middle of Shanghai. This was a meeting place for both buying and trading information on shares—some hundreds and often thousands of people gathered here every day. Because the retail clients' hall was small in those days, and hardware for the screen showing stock quotes had not yet been installed, many would-be investors had to climb over the fence and peer inside the windows to know what was going on.

Left: Seeking for 'wealth' on the street. Photo taken in July 1994.

Middle: Housing exchange meeting in 1989, at which citizens voluntarily came together to swap housing information.

Right: Peasant workers who haul things on their backs. Photographed in 1989.

took aim in the direction of reformers. The substance of the debate was condensed to one phrase, "Is it called socialism, or is it really called capitalism?!" Influenced by the insinuations, officials at all levels of government now found it hard to know what the proper line was. As a result, they began to vacillate and become paralyzed when it came to supporting further reform.

The mantle of history again fell upon Deng Xiaoping, who had long since announced he was retiring from the political scene. At first, he operated anonymously. From February 15 to March 22, 1991, the *Liberation Daily* in Shanghai published a series of three articles based on an address that Deng Xiaoping had made earlier. The content of the articles was not attributed to him, however, that information only came out later. The articles were entitled "Calming the Huangpu," for the river that flows between Shanghai and Pudong. They said that China should continue to adhere to liberated thinking, should be willing to take risks, carry on reform. China should not be constrained by some ongoing debate about whether it was called "socialist" or "capitalist." As soon as the articles appeared, they stirred up tremendous debate, particularly as the source of the thinking behind them had not been revealed. Some people therefore criticized and condemned the thinking and began to make "encircling attacks" around it. One article published on April 20 charged that, "Not asking if it is capitalist or socialist will simply lead us down a capitalist road." Another noted, "All Chinese people who are not willing to be enslaved yet again have a responsibility and a right to question whether it is called socialist or capitalist. At the same time, we need to make sure we do not deviate from the direction of reform."

The situation was clarified in a decisive manner in the springtime of 1992. From January 18 to February 21, Deng Xiaoping went on a "southern tour" of various places including Wuchang, Shenzhen, Zhuhai, and Shanghai. The name of this famous trip echoed the "Southern Inspection Tour" of the Emperor Kangxi in the year 1689, an event commemorated in a famous scroll painting that still exists. During Deng Xiaoping's southern tour, he delivered a series of famous "viewpoints" which were to guide the direction of China in the future.

These viewpoints were abbreviated statements that could be translated in various ways into English, but that generally were as follows. "The basic route of the Party will not change for one hundred years." "In determining the standards by which to judge our work, we should consider whether or not the result is beneficial to the productivity and growth of our socialist society. Is it beneficial to increasing the comprehensive national strength of our socialist country. Is it beneficial to raising people's standard of living." "The basic quality of socialism is to release productivity, develop productivity, eliminate exploitation, eliminate extremism. Its aim is finally to arrive at a common prosperity." "The fundamental distinction between socialism and capitalism does not lie in whether you have a little more Plan or a little more Market." "We must be a little braver in approaching reform and opening up. We must grasp the moment and develop ourselves. Of key importance is developing the economy." "China should be on guard against rightism, but even more importantly it should prevent leftism." "Firmly grasp hold with two hands, and both hands have to be hard and strong. Build up the "two civilizations," (referring to material civilization and spiritual civilization) for only this will create real socialism with

Wuchang in 1992. Wuchang was the first stop on Deng Xiaoping's 'Southern Tour.'

Chinese characteristics." These talks by Deng Xiaoping put a resounding "closure" on the ideological debate that had by then seeped into every aspect of life. Deng Xiaoping had no patience for any more discussion on a theoretical level about hazy and insignificant details.

On March 26, 1992, an article of 11,000 words in length was published in the *Shenzhen Special Economic Zone News*. It was titled, "An Eastern Wind Is Blowing in, Springtime Fills the Air: Comrade Deng Xiaoping commemorates his visit to Shenzhen." The next day, all newspapers carried this article in headline positions. In the past, such a momentous report would have been issued first and on a coordinated basis by the *People's Daily* or the Xinhua News Agency. The unusual nature of this release added to its impact. "Two meetings" convened in Beijing on the day after the article was published, so that the content of the article was very significant. Instantly, everyone fell in line with a rallying cry for an increase in the pace of reform and more liberated thinking. Any talk of whether such activity was socialist or capitalist faded away.

The Fourteenth Congress of the Communist Party was convened in October 1992, and clearly

GLOSSARY

Two meetings

China's two governing forums are colloquially called the "Two meetings," and are the National People's Congress and the Chinese People's Political Consultative Conference. These are held for around two weeks in March every year. A new "Congress" begins every five years, with the annual meetings in between called "plenary sessions."

The first bunch of stocks of Shanghai Companis, including Xiao Feile, Electronic Zhenkong, Yuyuan Department Store, Yan Zhong, and Shenhua Electronics.

spelled out goals of "establishing a socialist market-economy system." At the same time, the theoretical approach of "Building socialism with Chinese characteristics" was written into the Party bylaws. At the closing ceremony of the Fourteenth Congress, Deng Xiaoping shook hands with all attendees. His face wore a gentle smile. This was the last time the elderly gentleman was to appear at a Party Congress.

One dramatic episode at this juncture is worthy of note. After Deng Xiaoping journeyed south, the "heat wave" that followed was seen first in an explosion of the stock market. On August 7, 1992, the Shenzhen Exchange announced that it would be issuing five million vouchers allowing investors to subscribe to shares in new issues. Names of people who could subscribe to the new issues were to be chosen by lottery drawings at specific sites in the city. The selling of tickets for the vouchers was to begin in two days. Those who wanted to subscribe were required to show ID cards and each ID card would be allowed to get one ticket in the lottery. At most, each person could buy ten tickets at a time, using ten ID cards. In a one-time drawing, authorities would draw 500,000 valid tickets. Each ticket drawn then allowed a person to buy 1,000 shares of the companies going public.

The moment this announcement came out, a snowstorm

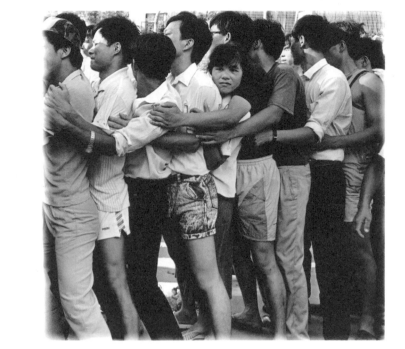

August 10, 1992, people lined up to buy lottery tickets for the chance to purchase shares that were being listed in Shenzhen. Pressed one up against another, they waited for two full days, only to find that most tickets had already been sold through illegitimate channels. The Shenzhen market at the time was notoriously corrupt.

August 10, 1992, in Shenzhen, when anger boiled over about inability to buy lottery tickets for share purchase.

A Slogan with Deng Xiaoping's decisive saying, 'The basic route of the Party will not change for one hundred years!' Photographed in Guangzhou, Guangdong, in 1993.

of the requisite identification documents began to bury the post office. Everyone in China was sending IDs to relatives or friends, to enable them to take part. They were also coming in person. Within two days, 1.5 million people were surging toward Shenzhen which at the time had a normal population of 600,000. It was soon impossible to get a train or bus ticket in to the city.

On August 8, early in the morning, long lines of people were sleeping on wicker mats stretched out behind the lottery-ticket sales points. By August 9, the streets and alleys of Shenzhen were seething with people. The lines at sales points were now six abreast. Shenzhen was awash in people with fistfuls of ID cards and currency notes, and with wild looks in their eyes. More than one million people had lined up at sales points. The municipal government held an emergency meeting and decided to print an additional allocation of tickets, to satisfy market demand.

Order soon broke down when ticket sales began. At some outlets, tickets were sold out two hours after opening since many had been sold earlier "through the back door" to insiders. Those who had been waiting for days and nights were now unwilling to leave. Some in the crowds began to shout in anger. The anger soon flowed into the streets in the form of

Left: December 1992, 'selling oneself,' i.e., trying to get a job at an employment exchange fair.

Reft: Mobicom was just starting in 1992, and cell phones were like small bricks at the time. They were therefore called 'brick-phones' in Chinese.

demonstrations as a charged mass of people moved like water in the direction of the municipal government. Shops were smashed, police cars were burned. The government mobilized the police force with high-pressure water hoses and the situation was brought under control.

One unexpected result of this incident was that the government was alerted to the extraordinary potential inherent in the capital markets. This led directly to the establishment of the Securities Regulatory Commission and a more orderly way of handling new issues. The voucher system was eliminated. China's markets faced a long bear market for some time after this, but the reforms were to prepare the way for eventual explosive growth.

If you were to divide China's reform and opening up process into two segments, the dividing line would come in 1992, a watershed in China's history. The speeding up of the pace of reforms in this year amazed many Western observers. It helped dispel an atmosphere of mistrust and misunderstanding that had pervaded the relationship between China and Western countries. Multinationals again started moving in the direction of China.

Jonathan D. Spence, a well-known Yale University Sinologist, has come to the conclusion that China's history can be

An impoverished mountain girl named Su Mingjuan, in 1991. She became the poster child for the 'Hope' cherity project.

read in terms of intersecting cycles of collapse and resurgence, revolution and advance, subjugation and development. The period from 1989 to 1992 was definitely such a "hand-over" in a cycle, a passing off of one cycle to the next. This period in the process of reform and opening up was highly sensitive but also thrilling. Under the stimulus of a market economy, all of China was like a child crazily growing in springtime. China's bones were cracking through old systems, old ways of thinking. The country seemed to be covered by one big invisible force, ceaselessly searching for a better ecological niche in which to grow upwards, outwards.

As one cycle ended and a new one began, China and its economy derived new life from amongst the cracks of the broken and discarded systems it was leaving behind.

PART THREE

Radical Dreams

1993–1997

Left page: July 26, 1996, Wang Junxia takes the championship in the 5,000-meter final at the Atlanta Olympics.

Upper: May 13, 2004, Wang Junxia photographed together with a photograph of her draped in the Chinese national flag after her victory in Atlanta.

Lower: 1996, China applies to hold the Olympics and unexpectedly fails. The photograph shows the disappointment in the faces of the Chairman of the Sports Commission, Rong Gaotang, and the host of the BTV program, as they hear the news.

Ruling over Chaos with an "Iron Wrist"

Chinese athletes broke two world records in 1993, and won a number of gold, bronze, and silver medals at the World Championships in Athletics in Stuttgart, Germany. It was an auspicious beginning to a new era in modern-day China. Even more significant as a symbolic change from the old days was

The testimony of the shortage of resources and materials in the planned economlg era: grain coupons, meat coupons, cloth coupons, coal coupons, etc.

the end to the system of food coupons. Representatives attending conferences in Beijing no longer had to hand over coupons to get their meals. On May 10, 1993, the Beijing municipal government formally announced that grain coupons were a thing of the past. The system had begun in 1955 and, for decades, everyone in China had used these rationed tickets to buy grain and other staples. Now, a symbol infused with the very taste of a "planned economy" disappeared from people's lives.

Other indicators made it clear in 1993 that China was no longer a planned economy in the traditional sense, and would not be again. Private business was brisk among regular people. That old term "speculation and profiteering" was no longer heard; what used to be a heinous crime was now part of normal daily life. Networks of local business economies were spreading like wildfire and, as a necessary part of any modern

On May 10, 1997, Beijing released the price of grains and edible oils from price controls. A salesperson at a grain store in the Chaoyang District of Beijing signs off on her last batch of grain coupons.

A photo of a family reunion in 1994.

market economy, capital markets were starting up as well.

On November 14, the Third Plenum of the Fourteenth Central Committee of the Communist Party passed a resolution called, "Decision regarding questions to do with establishing a socialist market-economy system." That month's issue of the *Economist* noted that, "Competition is spreading in all economic spheres in China. One factor is the expansion of foreign investment and foreign trade, another is that authority to make economic decisions is being pushed down to lower levels, leading to a rivalry among provinces that is amazingly like the economic reality of the federal system in the United States."

Zhu Rongji arrived in Beijing to assume duties as Vice Premier in 1991. Recommended for the post by Deng Xiaoping, he was specifically put in charge of the economy. Zhu had formerly served as Shanghai's Chairman of the Municipal Commission, so was highly experienced in economic management. For the next twelve years, he was to be in charge of guiding China's economic reforms as they went forward. His appointment signified that a new era of a strong authority at the helm had arrived.

Expert in enforcement, Zhu Rongji's first action was to clean up "triangular debt" as a way of establishing his command. For many years, in part due to the failure of "releasing prices" and

Beijing's *hutongs* disappear as the city remodels. The old buildings on Shenlu Street are just in the process of being demolished, outside Chaoyangmen, on December 16, 1994.

the consequent tightening of fiscal policies, enterprises had been loaning funds to one another. Professional courses on how to get loans were common in many areas. While one State-owned Enterprise waited to be paid for products it might have sold, or for loans it might have made, it was unable in turn to pay its own debts and bills. This resulted in a massive gridlocked situation. By 1991, this problem of "triangular debt" had reached a level of RMB 300 billion, of which 80% was owed by more than 800 large State-owned enterprises. In order to clean up triangular debt, Zhu Rongji first went to the three northeastern provinces where problems were most intractable, Liaoning, Jilin, and Heilongjiang. He person-

A small city in the mid-1990s, showing lots of people in narrow streets, everyone riding motorcycles to work.

ally took charge and personally went on site to clear things up. He proposed various measures to resolve the problems including an infusion of capital to start untying the linked debts, paying off debts with overstocked goods, structural adjustments, putting a strangle-hold on the source of any loaned funds, unlinking the chain of debt, and so on. Within

Left: 1994, a folk storyteller on the 'Majie storytelling fair,' Baofeng county, Henan Province.

Middle: A peasant worker washing the walls of a skyscraper in Shenzhen in 1997.

Right: Mother and daughter putting on make-up in front of mirrors.

twenty-six days, by ruling over a series of tough measures, he had cleared up RMB 12.5 billion worth of debt and the northeast issues were basically resolved. In the next half year, Zhu Rongji set time limits on clearing out remaining debts. He ordered compliance, and regional officials no longer had any place to hide. By May of 1992, a total of 4,283 fixed asset "projects" had been cleared up. Each input of 1 RMB from central coffers had cleared up 3.5 RMB worth of debt. The knots were untied and a problem that had wound itself around the Central and regional governments for years was finally resolved.

To a degree, the appearance of a man like Zhu Rongji at this time was a necessity. On the one hand, the economy had taken off like a stallion after Deng Xiaoping's journey to the south and his subsequent pronouncements. In 1991, construction underway in the country totaled about RMB 900 billion, by 1992 this had risen to RMB 2.2 trillion, and by May of 1993 it had risen another 69% on the previous year's base. The Central Bank put another RMB 50 billion of liquidity into the system, but all regions were crying for more money. On the other hand, supply and demand continued to be out of balance, the financial system was chaotic, and reform of State-owned enterprises was not making substantive progress. The *Economist* warned in an article in 1992, "At some point in 1993, the vibrant Chinese

1. June 16, 1994, the first group of 'peasant workers' from the Shanghai Peasant Workers' School gets off work. The surge of hundreds of millions of 'peasant workers' coming into cities is the source of the cost advantage of 'Made in China.' This labor migration is an important and often overlooked force behind the economic rise of China.

2. The annual movement of peasant workers from cities back to their homes at Spring Festival, and then back to the cities again, has been called the 'Spring Transportation.' It is a uniquely Chinese phenomenon. At train stations in cities like Guangzhou and Shanghai, workers frequently have to line up for several days and nights to board trains, meanwhile sleeping outdoors on the ground.

3. A tearful parting at the train platform between a young worker from Shandong named Liu Yong and his fiancée from Sichuan, Zhao Guihua.

4. The train station in Shanghai before the Spring Transportation in 1995.

5. A young boy from the countryside. Photographed in 1994, in Shuangbo County, Yunnan Province.

6. Young people head out to do menial labor, older people stay home in towns and villages. Photographed in 1995, in Guang'an County, Sichuan.

economy will face overheating. The last time was in 1988, when China almost caught fire." In the first half of 1993, prices of materials rose by 44.7%. Underground banks were extremely active, and unofficial "people's financing" rates went through the roof. The official interest rate stayed low, so those with connections, who could obtain official-rate money, loaned it out and made an instant 20% to 30%.

After Zhu Rongji's "First Battle" was completed, cleaning up triangular debt, he began his "Second Battle" in the realm of finance. He aimed at the illegal financing consortiums that were becoming more uncontrollable by the day. One company, for example, prided itself on investing only in high-tech companies. It put together RMB 1 billion in less than half a year. More than 100,000 common people loaned it money for the interest rates they could earn; some 93% of the investors were individuals. Soon, this consortium was involved in a crazy money-circle, charging and paying ever-higher rates. It quickly ran into wrong end of Zhu Rongji's rifle, who was at the time also serving as head of the Central Bank. The person involved was given the country's most severe punishment.

All reforms at any significant level eventually came back to the problem of how to divide up benefits. To those who were true reformers, this was the biggest test. In the end, in the face of tremendous opposition, Zhu Rongji proposed a reform of the way in which tax revenues should be split between national and provincial governments. He began going through the fiscal relationship between Central and local governments with a fine-toothed comb. For many years, the development of regional economies as well as State-operated enterprises had relied on infusions of funding from the central treasury. In the words of one economist, it was, "One old guy takes care of and pays for the upbringing of thousands of sons." The old guy was in a predicament, however, for if he relaxed controls, things became chaotic, while if he tightened up, his sons died. By the early 1990s, the national treasury was extremely short of money and relying on issuing large amounts of currency to make ends meet. This naturally brought on the risk of inflation. Some economists now suggested having central and

Old buildings about to be demolished in the 'golden area' of premier real estate in Beijing. Residents of the district being hurried out.

regional governments "eat at different troughs." They recommended having the Central Government and each province consult with each other on how to divide up tax revenues. The goal was to implement a division of taxation system and make local governments begin to rely on local sources for their funding.

Zhu Rongji officially proposed a division of taxation system for the first time to the national fiscal policy meeting on July 23, 1993. A little more than one month later, the first proposal in the reform came out. In order to persuade all provinces, Zhu Rongji personally spent the next two months going here and there, negotiating. There was much see-sawing and compromise in this process, but Zhu never wavered from the ultimate principle of implementing a "national unified tax division system reform."

The implementation of this reform forced the entire fiscal system of China into tremendous change. The results were sufficient to revive the finances of the Central Government.

Left: Luxury cars and high-fashion ladies are again seen on the streets in Shanghai, of great interest to Western photo-journalists.

Right: The first 'Healthy Sex Services Store' in China opens in Beijing in 1993.

From 1994 to 2002, China's treasury income rose on average by 17.5%. The ratio of tax income to GDP was 12.6% in 1993 rising to 18.5% in 2002. The ratio of central tax revenue to total government revenue was 55% in 2002, 33% higher than it had been before the reform in 1993. In 2002, other than assistance from tax refunds and structural help, the amount of payment paid out by the Central Government to regional governments in the form of "transfer payments" was as high as RMB 401.9 billion. This was 8.6 times the 1995 amount. Transfer payments in China refer to the practice by higher levels of government of paying out to lower levels of government a certain legislated standard amount of treasury receipts. This allocation is then considered a portion of "income" by local levels of government.

In addition to relying on the tax division reform to revive central finances, Zhu Rongji moved ahead with exchange-rate reform. He rejected all dissenting views, unified the system, and devalued the RMB. Before this reform, China had a two-track exchange system with both an official exchange rate and an adjusted regulated market rate. This was one of those tails that the governor of Sichuan had talked about, the "financial tail" of the planned economy. It both protected the benefit of State-owned enterprises, and it encouraged a tremendous black market in foreign-exchange transactions. From January 1, 1994, the two exchange systems were unified "onto one track," and a "single managed-float exchange rate system that used demand and supply as its basis for operations" was begun.

The RMB rate was initially set at RMB 8.72 to one US dollar.

Left: Border trade in the Northeast region is active.

Right: Beijing International Exhibition Center. An international textile equipment exhibition is under way and an older lady from Fengrun County in Hebei wanders through the crowds asking about this and that. Even though foreigners can't understand what she is saying, they are interested in the fact that she has attended the show.

The rate just before had been 5.7 to one, so this was an immediate devaluation of 33%. In 1978, the RMB to US rate was 1.7, in 1991 it was 4, in 1992 at the beginning of the year it was 5.7. This devaluation made Chinese products suddenly cheaper on the world market. Even more importantly, it allowed China to become a more attractive place to foreign investors. In Germany, a paper called the *Handelsblatt* noted that the devaluation meant that the four "Little Dragons" of Southeast and East Asia would now be losing their advantage of cheap labor. China would necessarily become the manufacturing center of the entire globe, and indeed that is what happened.

Zhu Rongji's "Third Battle" was aimed at State-owned enterprises. All previous reforms had focused on increasing the autonomy of the enterprises, but results were meager. If any industry had people-operated enterprises involved in it, then State-owned enterprise performance was bad, for the State-owned generally subsidized the people-operated for personal gain.

One place drew Zhu Rongji's attention for being different. A small county seat in Shandong called Zhucheng went further than any other in State-owned enterprise reform, and the experience of the local government could be summed up in one word, "sell." The thinking was very simple with regard

'Labor wanted.' Photographed in 1996, in Pingyuan County, Guangdong Province.

to State-owned small and medium-sized enterprises with poor results: lighten the load. Cast it off by complying with the directive of Central, which said, "Some State-owned small enterprises can be leased out or sold to collectives or to individuals for managing." The head of the county seat declared, "After ten years of reforming back and forth, enterprises were still resting in the same old embrace of the government. From today onwards, we are changing that relationship. From now on, it is 'you register, I record. You make money, I levy taxes. You get rich, I am happy. You break the law, I punish. You go bankrupt, I commiserate.'" As a result, through some seven different means including share-ownership system, share cooperative system, transfer of ownership for no compensation, and bankruptcy, this county sold 272 State-owned or collectively owned operations to individuals.

As Zhu Rongji saw it, the courageous action of this place deserved confirmation. The government could not initially deal with all State-owned enterprises by simply shaving them off, shaving the eyebrows together with the beard. This was because at the beginning of reform and opening up, there was no other force in the economy except for State-owned enterprises. If you did not rouse them to action then there was no hope for reviving the country. But today, township-and-village enterprises were springing up everywhere, privately-operated enterprises also were growing, while foreign-invested enterprises had swarmed into the picture. There was now an alternative commercial force to State-owned enterprises.

There was also now a tool for administering blood infusions into them, namely the two stock exchanges. Public listing could serve as an alternative to simple "allocations" by the treasury. Zhu Rongji recognized that under these new conditions, reform of State-owned enterprises would have to stop circling around the same old issues of operating systems. If one were to list State-owned enterprises on the stock exchanges, the central government would have to put considerable effort into totally restructuring them. This meant finally addressing the problem of who owned what.

Economists now came forward with a concept that was new to China. They argued that, "An ownership system should not be thought of merely in ideological terms, but rather as a means to developing productive capacity." Scholars buttressed this by saying that one should not grasp all enterprises to one's bosom forever, that it was not only unnecessary but it was also impossible. The country just needed to hold on to those most important, perhaps 500 to 1,000 of the large groups. This would release more breathing room for the small and medium-sized enterprises, while those that were not competitive or not necessary to the national economy and the people's livelihood could be "let go." The government could hold onto those that had potential to grow, that had resource advantages, were in strongly profitable industries, and were large.

Clearly, this was a way of thinking about reform that was radically different. It signified that reform of State-operated enterprises was shifting away from transfer of authority and in the direction of structural adjustments that involved "supporting the key ones and letting the rest go." A tremendous furor followed. After 2003, the results of this reform became quite apparent.

Around the year 1995, a number of famous entrepreneurs and brands arose in the areas of health-products and home electronics. Both of these business lines were controversial.

Price Wars

During the World Cup soccer games in the summer of 1994, CCTV broadcast a stirring advertisement in prime time that was a short 45 seconds, but effective. People saw ice breaking up on the Yellow River, heard Chinese gongs along the Great Wall, watched an Oriental-style lion proudly raise its head and roar at the sky. The images and wording of the ad were calculated to stimulate emotions. The whole thing served as a kind of collective oath of Chinese enterprises to charge forth and succeed.

'Health products' companies pursued a marketing strategy of blanketing the countryside with advertisements. The verb used was 'paste,' as in pasting ads on every wall, every telephone pole, every pigpen railing. The photograph shows an ad for a product called 'Heart K,' which was meant to 'fortify the blood.'

The charging began first with health beverages. Entrepreneurs in this industry often came from farming backgrounds but they were highly attuned to the psychology of consumers. Foreign brands had long been selling in China, as well as companies from Taiwan and Hong Kong, but these homegrown salesmen were masters of advertising strategies, sales networks, and price points. They quickly took over local markets throughout China with the creativity of the native-born in his own land.

The success of the health beverages entrepreneurs stimulated people to think that other industries could succeed in similar fashion. The economy was growing and domestic consumers were the target: there appeared to be an unlimited market that was not only expanding but apparently without limit. "Expand, expand again!" became the battle cry in all kinds of consumer industries. This sparked the first wave of diversification in China as companies blindly rushed to capture markets and grow through mergers and acquisitions.

As China's entrepreneurs were collectively putting out energy, multinational armies were marching into the country wearing steel-plated armor. In 1993, China entered the International Copyright Convention, and the Disney character that everyone already knew well, Mickey Mouse, or "Mi-Mouse" as he is known in China, formally and officially entered the country. Along with the smiling face of Mi-mouse, however, came the iron jaws and sharp teeth of multinational lawyers.

In 1993, Kentucky Fried Chicken opened its first outlet in the city of Xi'an, with a special operating permission. Procter and Gamble set up four companies and five factories in the same year, in one fell swoop. The world's largest beer company, Anheuser Busch, spent RMB 1.64 billion to purchase 5% of China's largest beer company, Qingdao Beer. Kodak sponsored the first East Asian Games in Shanghai, Nokia began to supply GSM mobile telephones to China, Citibank transferred its regional headquarters from Hong Kong to Shanghai. Boeing made a large amount of money off China in 1993 with an order for 120 planes that was said to be valued at USD 9 billion. The senior executive in charge of international business for Ford declared that his primary responsibilities related to China. Japanese investments in China grew rapidly in 1993. A total of 3,414 licenses were granted to Japanese companies to invest in

Left: GM automile came off the assembly line.

Right: 'Thank you, China. Made in U.S.A.' An interesting banner was hung up when 1,985 Chevrolet cars were imported from the U.S. to the port in Tianjin on August 7, 1993.

Chinese projects, which was three times the figure in 1991.

Most of the USD 346.2 billion in foreign investment that China attracted to her shores between 1979 and 2000 came after the year 1992. The amount from 1992 to 2000 represented 93% of the total. At the end of 1993, contracted foreign investment reached USD 111.4 billion, while actual use of foreign investment was USD 27 billion, which was double what it had been in the previous year.

Every multinational executive came to China with rosy-colored Oriental dreams in mind. The best example was none other than the CEO of Kodak. With great enthusiasm and confidence, he said, "If only half of China's population shoots one 36-exposure film in one year, that is already more than one-quarter of the world's annual demand. If 500 shots are taken every second in China, the total is equal to the entire Japanese and American markets." Multiplying the population by any given product to come up with the market was a calculation that virtually all multinationals did when entering China.

International investment was all to the good, but local Chinese companies soon found that they were facing heavy pressure from industries, like traditional home electronics, that came in backed by very substantial resources. Soon, a defensive action to protect Chinese industries on their home turf was called into action.

Liu Chuanzhi, founder of Lenovo, responded to a question about this in an interview. "It doesn't matter whether or not we are willing to take up the cause; we have *de facto* already become the flag-bearer for our native computer industry. At

For Chinese entrepreneurs to be seated on the dais together with world-famous executives indicated that Chinese entrepreneurs had begun to get some recognition, even though they still had a long way to go. This is the Chairman of the Board of the TCL Group, Li Dongsheng, together with Jack Welch, CEO of General Electric, speaking at a forum in China.

the very least we need to play for our lives. If we lose, then we go to our deaths like heroes." When the reporter asked further, "If China completely loses its own native industry, what is really so very wrong with that?" Liu Chuanzhi's eyes widened and he retorted, "What's wrong with it?! Nothing, just that we are sending our people to the slaughter." Soon after, this leading company in the Chinese computer industry was able to put out a machine that was priced at half of what foreign brands charged, by using extreme cost-cutting methods while maintaining the same functions.

In color televisions, TCL in Huizhou, headed by Li Dongsheng, similarly declared itself "willing to die in leading the charge." It started a price war at the huge electronics mart in Beijing. TCL's competition was from Japan, and its price was two-thirds of theirs. The color television manufacturer Changhong,

The Changhong Group in Sichuan was the largest manufacturer of color televisions in China in 1995. The Chairman of the Board, Ni Runfeng, was known for excelling at price wars, and he personally went behind counters to sell TVs.

based in Sichuan, joined in with the slogan, "We will build a new Great Wall with our brands." Changhong then slashed prices in ruthless fashion. "We deliver every function that a foreign product has; we have the whole product range that they have, any services they deliver, we provide as well. But for the same functions and the same quality, our prices are 30% lower." After bloodletting price cuts, this company was successful and became the reigning champion in the domestic market for color TVs.

Multinational companies had not imagined that their defeat would come at the hands of unforeseen price wars. GE was soon to face the same problem, and soon to lose as well. Based in Beijing, its GE Jiabao Lighting Company was never able to turn a profit. Thomas Edison may have invented the light bulb and the company may have made light bulbs for over one hundred years, but operating and manufacturing costs were high in China. GE was fundamentally unable to compete against small factories in Jiangsu and Zhejiang. One GE bulb with its soft light and eco-friendly components could be used for a full year but cost RMB 10. Domestic light bulbs had harsh light and could only be used a few months, but they cost a mere RMB 2. GE's market research finally had to admit, "Our light bulbs have better features, but Chinese look only at price."

The world's largest appliances company, Whirlpool, ran into even worse problems. In order to enter the China market quickly, Whirlpool adopted a mergers-and-acquisitions strategy. It found four companies with relatively good performance that made refrigerators, washing machines, microwaves, and color televisions. The matter was not as easy as it looked on the outside, however. One employee later recalled that a tall, bearded American was appointed general manager of one joint venture. He shut himself into an opaque glass-lined office from which streams of English would emerge, or occasionally a bizarre form of Chinese. The employee's task turned out to be to bring him coffee every once in a while. As a result, a large company with 14% of the world market in its products found that it was soon spending USD 500 million in China with nothing to show for it.

"The key to understanding the China market is patience!" Jack Welch, the world No. 1 CEO, was heard to say, as though this were the ultimate answer.

Limiting 'over-birthing' has always been one of the most important tasks of county- and village-level governments in China. Slogans and banners papered towns throughout China promoting birth control.

CCTV began to auction advertising rights to its primetime slots in 1994 and those who won were dubbed 'King.' For the next five or six years, this became the fastest way to make your brand famous, which led to irrational behavior on the part of those wanting to be King. The photo shows Shandong Qinchi Alcoholic Beverages Factory. Three years later, this 'King' was bankrupt.

Becoming One of the Fortune 500

In May of 1996, a book was published titled, *China Can Say No: the political and emotional choices in a post-cold war era.* Fifty thousand copies were printed, which sold out within twenty days. Five young college graduates, all under the age of thirty, had written the book. It raised strong doubts about the superpower status of America, so the American embassy in China soon invited the five to come for a talk. At the time, this was seen as a symbolic event by the Chinese public, since the tide of Chinese nationalism was running high.

A sense of radical optimism had been pervading the entire commercial world in China. People believed that miracles could happen, one could quickly create an empire. This was reflected in the prices paid for prime-time advertising on CCTV, determined at auction. One head of a business that produced alcoholic beverages was full of confidence as he bid RMB 321,211,800 for the "brand king" position. When asked by a reporter how he calculated this number, he replied happily, "I didn't calculate at all. It's just my telephone number."

China had reason to be proud at this moment. Everything looked promising. The consumer market was flourishing, local companies were full of vigor and passion. China's gradual-style reforms appeared to be successful, in contrast to the rest of the globe. The Russian economy to the north was mired down in serious problems. "Shock therapy," promoted in that country since 1992, with its rapid privatizing reform, had led to severe inflation and a downward sliding economy. In order to support the Yeltsin government, Western countries provided USD 10.2 billion in emergency aid. *Newsweek* noted, "A strong China is emerging and the country is now having a shocking influence in virtually all fields. From the Straits of Taiwan to the stores of America, none of this could have been foreseen when Deng Xiaoping began reform and opening up policies in 1979. As an economic power, China is not only entering but also changing the world's markets. It is sometimes even making up its own rules of the game." To many, the approaching footsteps of a "China century" could already be heard. Influenced by this optimism, the stock market index in Shanghai went from 537 at the beginning of 1996 to 1200 in November of that year.

The recovery of the Chinese economy was the result of the collective ascent of newly established enterprises. Old-brand and old-style State-owned enterprises had little to do with it and indeed had fallen off a cliff. What happened in Shanghai is a microcosm of the situation elsewhere. From 1990 to 1999, Shanghai steadily implemented a strategic urban transformation policy. It got rid of what were called old "second-wave" industries and brought in new "third-wave" industries. The policy was called

The return of Hong Kong and the economic revival brought a sense of patriotism to China. *China Can Say No* was one of the hottest titles in the late 1990s.

"Out with two, In with three." Old industrial enterprises were either disbanded or moved outside the city center, which was an extremely difficult and painful process. The textile industry was hit particularly hard. In total, 41 textile enterprises that were bankrupt were closed down, 200 other old enterprises were sold, what had been a total of 2.5 million cotton spindles was reduced to 700,000. Six hundred thousand factory workers were laid off, most of them female. During the 1990s, the unemployment rate in Shanghai increased at an average annual rate of 9.53%. The highest rate of increase was between the years 1990 and 1995, an increase of 13.17% every year, and this only included people who actually registered and recorded themselves as unemployed. The same thing went on in China's other old industrialized areas. It must be remembered that many tens of millions of employees of China's older enterprises paid a huge price for the reform of China's urban economies.

Meanwhile, State-owned enterprises in this period were clutching to grab what was known as the "last fistful of rice." The government had determined that the way to save these moribund entities was to restructure them and list a portion of their shares on the stock market as a way to spread the burden. "Listing on the market" was lucrative for those who could get a share allocation, hence the reference to the rice.

Not every entity was allowed to list; there was a quota. Once an enterprise had been approved as part of the quota, the State government in the form of treasury officials and bank authorities first turned what had been the "government allocations" to the enterprise into debt. It accounted for the amounts owed by turning the sum into bonds or various forms of debt instruments. It then turned those debt instruments into shares. Finally, through issuance of shares on the stock market, the government did everything in its power to sell the shares to shareholders.

This had two positive results. On the one hand, it allowed State-owned enterprises that were gasping for a final breath one more chance to start breathing again. On the other hand, it also resolved the so-called "tiger in the cage" problem. This

Shenzhen grows still taller. June 5, 1995, the 383.95-meter-tall Shenzhen Diwang Building is almost completed.

referred to the way Chinese savings were accumulating at a fast pace—instead of being put to productive use they were being hoarded away.

As the most dangerous period approached in terms of the survival of State-owned enterprises, the government's thinking turned about-face in a substantive way. The "blood transfusion" that certain State-owned enterprises were getting from the stock market gave them temporary support, but at the same time it turned the newly opened capital markets into a gamblers' paradise. In order to deal with several hundred thousand State-owned enterprises, the Central Government finally adopted a strategy of "keep hold of the big ones and let the little ones go." "Let the little ones go" meant adopting the experience of that town in Shandong called Zhucheng. "Keeping hold of the big ones" meant vigorous support for those State-owned enterprises that were charging into the market. The intent was to turn them into Fortune 500 companies as fast as possible.

In Chinese, the term "Fortune 500" is not actually used; a direct translation of the Chinese term is "The World's Strongest 500." The Chinese term was derived from the "Fortune 500," however, which is a list of names in *Fortune* magazine that ranks the world's largest corporations. The basis for the

From 1996, joining the Fortune 500 became the dream of many Chinese entrepreneurs.

ranking is sales turnover and market capitalization, and an updated list is announced in October every year. In 1989, the Bank of China became the first Chinese company to appear on the Fortune 500.

At that time, few people in China knew about this ranking and few cared about it. The idea of an annual sales volume on the order of billions of US dollars was so far out of the question that they dismissed it. In 1995, *Fortune* magazine broadened the scope of companies included in the ranking, and by this time Chinese companies were more aware of the prestige value of the list. Getting into the Fortune 500, or what in China continues to be known as the World's Strongest 500, became every Chinese entrepreneur's dream.

In 1995, Haier Company in Qingdao declared that it intended to be among the Fortune 500 by the year 2006. Within six months, at least thirty other Chinese companies set out the same sort of timetable. The Fortune 500 gradually became a kind of mystical totem, a Holy Grail deeply embedded in the collective unconsciousness of China's entrepreneurs.

The State Economic and Trade Commission soon announced that it would be extending key support to six specific companies in the years to come. These were Baosteel, Haier, Jiangnan Shipyard, North China Pharmaceutical, Founder, and

Changhong. The government would be doing everything it could to enable these companies to enter the ranks of the Fortune 500 in the year 2010. These six companies had a number of features in common. They included backing by State-owned capital, proven ability to be competitive in their markets, and leadership by a superlative entrepreneur.

Once the Central Government announced this "National Team," each province began to contend for attention with its own list. Each jostled for position, declaring that in a certain number of years its companies too would be joining the Fortune 500. The same thing occurred at local levels, with the goal to become one of the Top 100 in a given province. A movement began that was tied in to the goal of the Fortune 500, but that also mobilized the entire country to "grasp the strategy" of putting Chinese companies on the map.

This movement occurred at a peak of economic development in Asia, and the Korean company Daewoo was regarded as the overall model to emulate. Due to strong Korean government support, Daewoo had gone from being a small trading company with registered capital of only USD 10,000 to becoming a shockingly huge conglomerate in the space of thirty years. Its corporate structure was of intense interest to Chinese enterprises, for it combined manufacturing industries with financial entities. As many saw it, Korea's "eastern methods" were appropriate for and could be transplanted to China. Among policy makers and academic circles at the time in China, it was simply accepted common knowledge that China would be cultivating super-large enterprise "groups" that could rank with the Fortune 500. People felt that creating such "mother ships" was the best way to stand up against international competition. At that time, such super-large conglomerates could be regarded as a kind of symbol of China's economic ascent.

The dream of entering the Fortune 500, and the so-called Daewoo model, pushed the wave of diversification to a new height. Every industry had irresistible business opportunities in it. People could not wait to expand, and expand yet again. Entrepreneurs had not learned to curb their appetites and

In the mid-1990s, a class of people arose who specialized in making fake products, or knock-offs. These people were called 'diao-min' in Chinese, or hucksters. This man, Wang Hai, from Shandong, was a famous such huckster. He is shown with the fake cell phones he discovered in Chengdu, Sichuan.

eventually had to eat the consequences.

The phenomenon was most pronounced in the home electronics industry. After beating out competition from multinationals, local home electronics companies swiftly fell into a brutal form of "civil war." The weapon used had to be price, since the level of technology of all these companies was basically the same. Along with the price war, however, companies engaged in a "conceptual war" in which each loudly trumpeted its "technological transformation." In the years to come, China's electronics enterprises announced revolutionary technological breakthroughs with great regularity. Some declared that their refrigerators complied with Green standards, for example, and therefore tried to charge RMB 200 more for what had cost RMB 10.

State-owned enterprises in this industry swore that they were setting up new-technology centers. Later, people were amazed to discover that these so-called R&D centers were merely copying other products. New technology was absent, but new ideas abounded, and they were often ludicrous. Haier invented a new machine for washing sweet potatoes, for example. Later, as a result of research into consumer demand the company put out machines for washing lobsters. The media was able to make great fun of this, and the case study was even put into university course materials. In the end, this kind of "new product generation" led State-owned enterprises down the road of copying the form but not the substance. Rather than creating new technology, they were emptied of technology. China became the world's largest manufacturing base for electronics, but even today it is unable to make a product that is one-hundred-percent "Made in China." The high-tech components for color televisions, refrigerators, and air-conditioning units, for example, come from elsewhere.

As the craze to diversify rolled across China, entrepreneurs seemed to have lost the ability to sit quietly and conscientiously and create a new product. "I figure Chinese people are in too much of a hurry," noted Kenichi Ohmae, the Japanese management guru. "There are too many opportunities in China, to the point that businessmen find it hard to focus on just one area. Focusing is the only way to make money however, being outstanding in one area. Coca-Cola dedicates itself to producing carbonated beverages, and is therefore leader in the field. Toyota focuses on producing cars, and has become the most profitable company in Japan. The only way is to go into an industry, focus on it and become professional in it, and then globalize." He added, "China's entrepreneurs are thinking that they can accomplish in five years what it has taken Japan to do in fifty. This is a big mistake on the part of China. Management is a process of interconnected feedback loops. It's organic. If you try to base it on intensive straight-line analysis and prematurely take action, it's like trying artificially to manufacture a child."

Events were to prove that the collective dream of joining the Fortune 500 was a kind of youthful enthusiasm. The dream was soon to be thoroughly doused by the Asian financial crisis. Before that time, however, few in China could hear the message of Kenichi Ohmae.

As commerce flourished, China experienced an 'emptying out' of spiritual and cultural values. The T-shirt of this young man reads: 'Go with your feelings.'

Left: Deng Xiaoping had promised that he would personally go to Hong Kong when it was returned to China. His death preceded the date of Hong Kong's return by 131 days.

Right: Deng Xiaoping was cremated on February 24, 1997. Hundreds of thousands of people lined the streets to accompany what in Chinese is called the 'spirit-car.'

Unexpected Changes

The senior statesman Deng Xiaoping passed away on February 19, 1997, at the age of 93. He did not live to witness the return of Hong Kong to China, which happened less than five months later. On July 1, 1997, the British slowly lowered a Union Jack that had waved for a full century over the island of Hong Kong.

Just as Chinese were happily intoxicated by the return of Hong Kong, however, a storm was brewing that was soon to break over Asian countries.

It began in Thailand. The economy of Thailand was seriously overheated and the government was deeply in debt. In February, an American investor named George Soros led his Quantum Group in its first attack on the Thai currency by selling it in quantity. This caused the Baht to drop sharply in value against the US dollar. The Thai government used USD 5 billion of its dollar-denominated foreign reserves and another $20 billion in US dollar loans to try to prop it up. The Baht continued its downward slide. On July 2, the Thai government was forced to announce that the Baht was going on a free-floating system, and it immediately lost 20% in value. Swift attacks on

the Malaysian, Phillipine, and Indonesian currencies soon followed. Within four months, the middle classes of these three countries lost 50%, 61%, and 37% respectively of their asset values. South Korea was next. Faced with attack, the Korean currency lost 50% of its value in two months, the national economy appeared to be at the verge of collapse, and the company that had so recently been seen as a model to follow by Chinese entrepreneurs, Daewoo, simply toppled over.

Although China's system had control mechanisms with regard to international capital, and the country was not directly affected by the storm, it was indirected influenced by the economic decline of its neighbors. The Chinese stock market fell and consumers stopped buying. As the threat of inflation declined daily, the trick became to stimulate the economy again. Interest rates on loans approached zero, but this still did not stimulate consumption or production. According to a report put out by the State

July 1, 1997, Hong Kong is returned to China and the shame a century is washed away in the space of one day.

The 'finance crocodile,' George Soros, who contributed to the Asian financial crisis of 1997. For the first time, China displayed the form and the substance of an economic power during this crisis. At the same time, China turned on a dime in modifying its domestic economic policies.

Upper left: The construction of the Three Gorges dam greatly changed the face of cities in central Sichuan. The erection of stone markers reading '156 meter water line' presages the fact that by 2003 this area will be inundated by water. Photographed in 1997.

Upper right: Three Gorges immigrants.

Statistical Bureau, in mid-1997, the value of goods in inventory all over China exceeded RMB 300 trillion. There now seemed to be a phenomenon of "structural oversupply," supply greater than demand in 95% of all categories of industrial goods. This kind of over-stocked phenomenon had happened only once before, in 1990. In June of 1997, three government agencies came together to set up a Center for adjustment of national inventories. This soaked up some of the over-supply in an effort to get the economy moving again.

These extreme changes in the market environment meant that people-operated enterprises in China went into a landslide decline. Some enterprises that had been highly popular now were out of business. History is never the straight line that people expect—more commonly, it forks at the most unexpected times and presents people with extreme challenges. What nobody could have expected was that the Asian financial crisis, and China's resulting grim economy, allowed the "marketization"

October 23, 1997, three months after Hong Kong is returned to China, the stock market plunges by 1211 points, and newspaper headlines all scream, 'Stock market crashes.'

Graduates of higher education, just entering 'society,' enter the 'explosion' of the Shenzhen employment market. From 1997 on, the employment of college graduates in China was completely 'socialized,' meaning the State no longer assigned students to a position, 'society' created positions and students applied for jobs themselves.

of China's State-owned enterprises to surge ahead.

In point of fact, these State-owned enterprises had reached a point where they were either going to change or die. In January of 1997, a third annual survey of China's industry was published, with statistics that showed the situation was dire. The rate of return on capital in State-owned enterprises was only 3.29%, much lower than the interest rate on one-year bank deposits. Eighteen of thirty-nine industries were showing losses in the industry as a whole. Total debts of State-owned industry were 1.92 times equity—there were not enough assets in any enterprise group to offset its debts.

Township-and-village enterprises likewise were hitting a wall. In the past twenty years, two models had run neck-and-neck with each other. One was known as the "Wenzhou model," a privately initiated and privately owned form of enterprise. The other was known as the "Su-nan model," the prevailing form of collective enterprise in southern Jiangsu province. From around the mid-1990s, however, the collective-enterprise model began to be infected with many of the ills of

Left: In 1996, cell phones were considered luxury items, but soon their status dropped as everyone began using them. Even a vegetable seller had one in her pocket.

Right: 1997, a horsecart juxtaposed against a truck and a plane that is just about to land.

State-owned enterprises. The main reason was that ownership was not clearly delineated. One official openly described the problems in a speech. "The ownership structure [of collectively held township-and-village enterprises] is too uniform, division of responsibilities between government and enterprise is unclear, ownership of enterprise assets is not specified, and the previous vitality of these organizations has greatly diminished. Essentially, collectively owned township-and-village enterprises have turned into the same thing as the old system. What's worse, leaders in many areas are holding onto the model [out of self-interest], and not letting go. They are actively obstructing a more vital form of economic structure from developing."

This speech was later seen as a kind of collective introspection by officials regarding the Su-nan model. The "policy halo" that once surrounded Su-nan model now began to dissipate. By the end of 2002, by undergoing all kinds of "reforms," 90% of township-and-village enterprises in the Su-nan region had been turned into privately-operated enterprises. This marked the end of a long trajectory that had begun with experimental cooperatives in the 1950s. The People's Cooperative system that grew from the experiment finally molted into a form of publicly-held collective ownership of commercial entities in the 1990s. Collectively owned enterprises were still subject to the structural problems of State-owned enterprises, however, and this was now being recognized by policy-makers. This particular trajectory in China's commercial history was coming

to an end. A market-driven enterprise system that was characterized by concrete ownership rights was finally becoming main stream.

On September 12, 1997, at the Fifteenth National Congress of the Communist Party of China in Beijing, Jiang Zemin, the General Secretary, made a major revision in the theoretical underpinning of the traditional system of public ownership. He raised the concept of a "mixed-ownership" system. Not only that, but he indicated that the non-publicly owned part of the economy was already not just "supplementary" but in

Upper: A fashion show on the Golden Bridge in front of Tian'anmen Gate, in 1986.

Lower left: A fashion show in 1994.

Lower right: Fashion show.

fact "an important component part." He emphasized that just because the State-owned portion of the economy was declining, this would not overly influence the nature of socialism. Moreover, he declared an end to the debate on whether or not State-operated enterprises would or would not carry out asset-ownership reform.

This statement by Jiang Zemin and the proceedings of the Fifteenth Congress were seen as the start of a third great epoch of "thought liberation" in China. In 1998, a very influential book was published in China that described this third epoch, as well as the first two. It was written by the highly respected author, Ling Zhijun, and the editorial writer of the *People's Daily*, Ma Licheng. It was called *Crossing Swords: a record of three periods of thought liberation in modern China*. The first "sword fight" had been in 1978, and was about the standards by which to judge truth; the second was in 1992, about whether it was called "capitalism" or whether it was called "socialism." This was now the third. The opening of the Fifteenth indicated that China had finished the sword fight and started on a third epochal period of "thought liberation."

Now that the "thinking" had been clarified, the government began to wield a sharp knife. It began the process of "holding onto the big ones and letting the little ones go." Not unexpectedly, in actual implementation the thinking now began to take more proverbial twists and turns. Before this, the idea of "holding onto the big ones" had been to support certain enterprises and turn them into large financial groups, so that they could be internationally competitive and represent China's power and interests. Now, faced with the precarious nature of similar Korean and Japanese groups, the central government began to wonder. Given revelations of the internal weaknesses of Asian companies, during and after the financial crisis, the central government in fact lost confidence in this path. If Daewoo was unable to withstand the attack of international financial capital, how could China's Daewoo-like companies escape the same fate?

And so, a new strategy appeared. This was summed up as "State out, People in." Its basic thinking was that State-owned

capital should get out of completely competitive situations. Experts proposed that State-operated enterprises should "resolutely retreat from" 164 competitive industries. At the same time, the government should stay in strategic resource-type industries by adopting a strongly monopolistic posture. These industries included steel, resources, automobiles, airlines, telecommunications, electricity, banks, insurance, media, large-scale equipment, and munitions. In these industries, the government should do all it could to exclude all people-operated

Upper left: A wedding in 1987.

Upper right: 1997, a wedding in a *hutong* in Beijing.

Lower: 1997, cross-national wedding, i.e., a mixed marriage.

and internationally funded competition. Through forceful monopoly, the government should protect the vested interests of State-operated enterprises, it should be the owner of State-operated capital, and its role in these enterprises should not be weakened but instead should be strengthened. The confirmation of this national policy had a decisive influence on China's economy and on the way in which these major State-owned enterprises were to mature.

Part Four

Swamps and Landmines
1998–2002

Some Hairpins

China's two governing forums are colloquially called the "Two Meetings," and are the National People's Congress and the Chinese People's Political Consultative Conference. These are held for around two weeks in March every year. A new "Congress" begins every five years, with the annual meetings in between called "plenary sessions."

Zhu Rongji was appointed Premier at the First Plenary Session of the Ninth Congress, held in 1998. On March 19, at around 10:30 am, the new Premier took questions from a television journalist. He declared, "Responsibilities are heavy upon us in this next session. I feel the enormity of the task. I hope that I can meet the hopes and expectations of the people. No matter whether the ground ahead of us is strewn with landmines, or blocked by miles of impassable swamps, we will go forward. We will not look backwards. We will bend our backs to the work in front of us and die before we give up."

This talk of landmines and endless swamps placed China's reforms in forbidding territory. China had been through twenty years of reform, and the time had come to show more progress. Zhu Rongji made a promise to the people that within the

The People's Liberation Army rescued 'David's deer' as they stood on dikes surrounded by water during floods in 1998.

next four years he would accomplish three things. First was to preserve the value of the RMB and not devalue it. Second was to revive the economy by mobilizing domestic demand, and third was to enable State-owned enterprises to emerge from their problems within three years. This last appeared virtually impossible at the time, but a reform of real significance was indeed in the works.

Zhu Rongji's most pressing matter was to preserve the value of the RMB. At the beginning of 1998, the great "crocodile" George Soros, among others, is believed to have decided to attack the Hong Kong dollar, to which the RMB was tightly linked. At the time, given the handover to China in 1997, Hong Kong was in the midst of a panic with real estate prices falling and many thinking of leaving. Soros allegedly began his "sniping action" in the context of this panic. Within one day, international speculators now sold short more than 20 billion Hong Kong dollars, with the expectation that such an action would bring about a fall in price, at which time they would buy in again and reap the profit. The Hong

Floods along the Yangtze River in 1998.

Kong Monetary Authority "gnashed its teeth," and used its Exchange Fund to intervene. The message to speculators was clear: the Hong Kong government would not allow an attack on its currency and would become a player, a key player, in assuring stability. Speculators were attacking the stock market as well as the currency. The Hang Seng index fell to 6600, a decline of nearly 10,000 points from one year earlier, evaporating 2 trillion Hong Kong dollars' worth of market capitalization. On the decisive day of battle, August 12, 1998, the Hong Kong government finally held the market and succeeded in stabilizing the situation.

Hong Kong was able to withstand the pressure of international speculators because it enjoyed the support of the central government of China. China had made it clear that it would stand firm in the face of financial instability one year earlier at a key World Bank meeting.

In October 1997, the World Bank held its annual meeting in Hong Kong, and Soros, Mahathir, the Prime Minister of Malaysia, Chubais, the Prime Minister of Russia, among others, were invited to attend. Given the ongoing Asian financial crisis, no-one knew if the RMB was going to be devalued or not. This was perhaps the most sensitive issue facing attendees. The World Bank invited Zhu Rongji to give the keynote speech, and in his remarks, he solemnly declared, "China will adhere to the position of not devaluing the RMB. It will take on the historic responsibility of stabilizing Asian finance." All leaders of Asian states drew a long breath when this sentence was uttered. The *Far Eastern Economic Review* later noted, "For the first time, China is playing the role of a major economic power in meeting an economic crisis of a global nature."

Zhu took an unprecedented risk in deciding to defend the RMB. China's economy was flagging and the country could little afford to play the hero. Exports were declining, inventories of over-stocked goods were rising, consumer demand was listless. In June, hundred-year floods raged along the Yangtze River basin. Twenty-nine provinces were severely affected, 4,150 people died, and direct economic losses came to RMB 255.1 billion. It was universally understood that if China did

The system of 'housing as a social benefit' was abolished in 1998 and people began to be allowed to get mortgage loans to purchase their own homes. As a result, a housing boom began that has been the engine behind China's economic growth for the past decade. Housing construction has also been the industry with the most 'explosive profits' in the country. The photograph shows an advertisement for housing.

A view from behind.

not devalue its RMB, its economy would be in serious trouble.

The only possible course of action was to "turn the eyes inward" and stimulate domestic demand. Chinese people lead the world in their propensity to stash away savings. Some RMB 5 trillion was locked away in savings deposits at that time—if just some of this could be diverted to consumption and released into the economy, an economic recovery would follow. Zhu Rongji made what, at the time, was a very momentous decision. In order to stimulate consumption, he decided to promote the buying and selling of real estate. In recent years, he had recommended policies that restrained the development of real estate. In order to prevent inflation, he felt he had stay on guard against the speculative behavior that the real estate market could foster. Today was different. To mobilize domestic demand, the only weapon in his arsenal was housing.

For more than forty years, housing had been allocated to each and every Chinese person in the country as a social benefit. It was allocated via the "units" or organizations to which people were assigned. In July of 1998, the State Council put an end to this system. It determined that all Party and government organizations would cease to distribute housing and instead would promote the monetization of housing allotments. The adoption of this policy meant that there was suddenly a vast market for housing in China.

At about the same time, the State Council announced it was "going a step further in deepening reforms of the housing system as applied to cities and towns, and was speeding up the construction of housing." The housing supply system would now "take economic-use housing as its core," a euphemism for purchased housing. The People's Bank of China then issued regulations on housing loans. The policy permitted commercial banks to begin offering mortgage loans, and permitted borrowers to pay back on the basis of interest-only or interest-and-principle. The new policies were highly effective in stimulating the economy. China began a real estate boom that has lasted now for over ten years. Countless stories of sudden wealth have been generated in the process.

Since the housing industry was tightly linked to a broad network of other industries, the new policies were especially helpful in stimulating such areas as steel, cement, and other resources. Economists were later to confirm that, "The policy was a turning point in market demand after the Asian financial crisis. The impact has persisted over the course of a full decade. Consumer loans stimulated demand for housing. Large-scale infrastructure projects stimulated demand in the financial markets. Many enterprises were able to expand significantly with the infusion of capital. Since investment funding was available, those industries in energy supply and basic materials were able to maintain steady growth. This provided an excellent market environment for the State-owned enterprises that were the source of raw materials and energy inputs."

Zhu Rongji had promised that within three years he would enable State-owned enterprises to emerge from their problems. This undoubtedly was the most difficult of his three commitments. In 1998, the reality was that, as the Ministry of Finance reported, State-owned enterprises frequently filed false reports as a way to cover up their very serious straits. The Ministry conducted a survey of one hundred key State-owned enterprises in the years 1997 and 1998. The results showed that 81% of enterprises reported assets that were "non-existing" and profits that were "empty, i.e., false." Nobody explained why

The Chinese Goverment agree to Kodak's suggestion of buying China's entire film industry in 1998. This had generated much disputes. Photographed were Premier Zhu Rongji and the CEO of Kadak, George Fisher.

this was the case, but everyone knew: since they belonged to the people at large and nobody was responsible for the consequences, State-owned enterprises had been gutted.

Five days after the speech in which he mentioned landmines, Zhu Rongji signed off on what looked like a crazy plan. The Chinese government agreed to allow the largest photographic film company in the world, Kodak, to come in to China and buy up its entire film industry. The industry was made up of seven Chinese enterprises. According to the agreement, these were to be incorporated into a joint-venture company with Kodak. Kodak promised to invest USD 1 billion, and to bring the world's premier photo-sensitive technology to China. This shocking news soon came to be called the "'98 Agreement."

The photographic film industry in China could serve as a mirror to all other State-owned enterprises. Like the home electronics and beverages industries, the film industry "reformed" after 1978 and began to import complete production lines. Starting in the 1980s, all regional governments competed for "projects." This term "project" in Chinese signifies an economic activity that has been approved by the government and that is funded by the government. With government funds, therefore, regional governments began to import equipment for making film from Fuji, Kodak, and the German company

Agfa. Among these, Xiamen's investment in Kodak imports totaled RMB 1.5 billion, Shantou's investment in Fuji imports totaled RMB 4 billion. In the short space of ten years, China established seven film-making factories, making it the most film-intensive country on the globe. All of the chronic illnesses of State-owned enterprises were exhibited in the film industry. These included massive duplication in investments, inability to absorb technology, inability to be competitive in the market, rigid management mechanisms, and, especially, "chaotic" management. This latter referred in part to the possibility that "managers" were able to take a certain percentage of investment in management fees. By around 1993, all seven film factories were making a loss and the industry's debt exceeded RMB 10 billion. Faced with this situation, even Zhu Rongji, the maestro at managing chaos, was at a loss as to how to begin.

Kodak's plan took shape as early as 1994. In the fall of that year, George Fisher , the CEO of the company met with Zhu Rongji at the Western Lake in Hangzhou. When this CEO raised the idea of buying China's entire film industry, everyone listening in to the conversation was amazed. It had not been discussed in advance, and even the senior Kodak people accompanying the CEO were hearing it for the first time. Zhu Rongji was alone in not thinking that the "heavens had split open." He was calculating his next move on the *weiqi* (go) board in his mind.

Kodak's proposal was tempting. The company would bring three things to the table that could have a positive impact on reform of the State-owned enterprises involved: technology, world-class management, and at least USD 1 billion. At the same time, Kodak demanded exclusivity. "We ask that no other foreign competitor be allowed to enter China," the company explained, "We have to reorganize the existing enterprises but they are able to build new factories." This thinking tallied exactly with what was needed in China. The reality was that the government had little ability to deal with the problems. Zhu Rongji decided to take the risk, and to begin at the earliest possible time.

Handing over an important industry into the hands of

a multinational company was an unheard of way of doing things in China. For one thing, the purchase of an entire industry would rewrite its traditional "benefits" structure. It would "annihilate the forces" of the previous "people's industry." From start to finish, Zhu Rongji was a supporter of merging and acquiring the industry. As a result, he was soon called a traitor to his country for "letting the wolf in the door."

He faced these charges with great aplomb. "Some people ask if it won't change the nature of socialism to decrease the proportion of State-owned to privately-held portions of an enterprise. The key thing is maintaining the economic lifeline, the blood of the system. A few hamburgers, some rolls of film, some hairpins—if you bring in a little foreign investment with these, what difference does it make?" The reference was to Kodak.

The Kodak proposal went forward, signifying that China's central government was taking another historic step with regard to reform of State-owned enterprises. The year 1998 represented a major dividing line. The focus before this time was on changing "operating mechanisms." After this, it was on restructuring and clarifying ownership. The results of early reforms might have been modest, but government policy was always extremely clear. Now, the results were quite outstanding but government policy remained intentionally vague. It was first expressed in the slogan "reform, reorganization, renewal." After that, a rousing movement called "State out, People in" was promoted. As a result, a tremendous restructuring was completed within a few years. One important thing to note is that a group of large State-owned enterprises that had been failing were, as a result, turned into a kind of invincible fleet.

Those enterprises that were subjected to the "State out, People in" policy underwent a restructuring of ownership and ceased to be part of the fleet. In this process, however, people who had been in charge of these enterprises were allowed to assume control over vast wealth. This has elicited unending debate in recent years. The process went forward at all levels of government, local, provincial, and national, and was known in colloquial parlance as the "last banquet." The "State out, People

Starting in 1990, China started holding experimental elections for the lowest level of administrative officials, Chair of the Village Commissions. This photogrph shows the public calling out votes as they are counted in Leikou Township, Anyang County, Henan Province, in October 1998.

in" policy was an "unspecified, generalized movement," which is to say it lacked precise legal parameters and regulatory oversight. In the course of changing ownership, how certain individuals assumed control over assets is rather unclear. Much of this is and will forever remain a mystery. Some of the names that later began to appear on the list of "China's Richest" were undoubtedly recipients of the benefits of this latest round of reform.

Started in around 1998, lottery tickets ignited the hopes and desires of many lower- and middle-class people. The activities surrounding the drawings were often attended by hundreds of thousands of people in many cities.

From 1998 onward, China's reform entered a stage in which the distribution of benefits was more complex and the conflicts were more violent. From policy-making authorities to entrepreneurs to intellectuals, everyone now felt that reform had been pushed into unknown territory. People began to feel a desire to resist what was happening in their own lives, as well as a sense of helplessness about where the country was going. In the years after 1998, people came to understand far more clearly what Zhu Rongji had referred to when he mentioned "landmines" and "swamps."

Authority over Macao was transferred from Portugal to the People's Republic of China on December 20, 1999, which brought an end to over one hundred years of colonialism in that territory.

The Birthing of the Stock Market, and Its Chronic Problems

A century that had caused so much confusion and so many conflicts finally came to its end in 1999. To mark the transition to a new century, one that many Chinese are calling "China's Century," *Fortune* magazine announced that it was going to be holding its annual meeting in Shanghai. It scheduled the meeting for the end of September, prior to the country's large national holiday. This was the first time a famous media organization had selected China to be the site of its global annual meeting. The topic was in line with everyone's thinking: "Let the world understand China and let China understand the world."

Environmental degradation increasingly impacts cities in China. Starting in 1988, sandstorms became an environmental hazard in Beijing.

This was a comforting approach to China's increasingly close ties to the rest of the world. China's macro-economic performance was also bringing comfort to many quarters. The country was like a "lone ranger" in leading economic development. Southeast Asia had still not recovered from its financial debacle, further crises had erupted in Russia and Brazil. China, in contrast, was responding to policy measures. The consumer market had revived and the booming housing market was drawing all sectors along with it in a cycle of new, fast growth.

Meanwhile, the capital markets were taking their own course. In most of the world, the capital markets have always been a barometer of the economy, but in China this "barometer" frequently played jokes on people, like some kind of funny distorting mirror in a carnival.

May 19, 1999, started as a normal day, a day unworthy of any kind of major news. The stock markets had been listless for more than 700 days in a row, but on this day they suddenly woke up. A succession of thirty-two days of positive news had allowed a ray of sunshine finally to break through. The Central Bank had lowered interest rates, but more importantly a new Securities Law had been passed. The normally cautious *People's Daily* now published a special editorial on May 19, asking everyone to "have firm confidence, respect the new regulations, enjoy the positive situation in the stock markets." Within two months, the Shanghai exchange had shot up by 1700 points, an increase in market capitalization of more than 50%. Shareholders reveled in the long-awaited sunshine.

Another group of people, however, now came out of their lairs with a great shout of joy. This was the clever, risk-taking class of people that in China are known as *"zhuang-jia."* The word "speculators" does not do them justice. The term *zhuang-jia* dates from the old gambling days of China, when these people served as bankers in the game and held all the chips in their hands.

In the contemporary Chinese capital markets, this noxious weed called *zhuang-jia* arose as a result of the system. Sickly State-owned enterprises that had to be "released from their problems" by going public were the first factor allowing *zhuang-jia* to exist. Not long after these enterprises went public, their finances quickly deteriorated, the money evaporated, and

The Shanghai Stock Exchange has been dubbed a 'gambling den' by economists. 'Zhuang-jia' or manipulative operators hide behind a variety of screens. The greatest losers, the 'sacrificed,' are the little shareholders.

they again fell on hard times. This led to their being referred to as "shells" for sourcing capital. A second systemic cause of the existence of these speculators was the dual-nature of the Chinese stock market in its early years. When the market was set up, due to "defects in systems design," a strange situation existed that allowed two different classes of shares to be issued. One could be traded and the other could not. Generally around two-thirds of the shares could not be traded, so that these non-traded shares held a controlling position. Traded and non-traded shares therefore had different amounts of power: the power of non-traded shares could be used to manipulate the market for traded shares. Meanwhile, the enforcement structure of listed companies was extremely "deficient." It was very easy to have a "dominant shareholder" and even an "autocratic shareholder." The existence of non-traded shares allowed *zhuang-jia*, in alliance with key shareholders or as the key shareholders themselves, to use extremely cheap and "grey" measures to control a company. The immaturity of regulatory mechanisms meant that there was no way to prevent people from manipulating the stock price for private gain.

For a long time, the most popular noun in the Chinese stock market was *"ti-cai,"* which means subject matter. All you had to do was dream up rumors and scares and false information, and be brave enough to undertake all the tricks, and you could easily succeed in this business.

Zhuang-jia frequently had the following characteristics. First, they were, without exception, exceptionally good at making up stories. Among a widely dispersed group of shareholders, not privy to real information, the little shareholders were as lambs to the slaughter. Because of the extreme information asymmetry, the *zhuang-jia* often hid in the background, behind the scenes, from whence they threw out scraps of eye-opening "material." In this, the media played a complicit role. Often paid for their services, journalists were able to weave fabulous stories around certain shares and to manufacture miracles on behalf of the speculators. Secondly, *zhuang-jia* were highly talented in using capital to their advantage. As they saw it, there was not a more profitable place in the world than a stock market. They used "shell capital sources" that had a name but no substance to serve as buyers, as well as legal-person non-traded shares of State-owned enterprises that were already listed. From these blinds, they would be able to buy in at a cheap price, and in short order create an empire that did more in managing finances than in managing any real business.

One former *zhuang-jia* will serve as a case in point. At his height, he controlled the shares of three companies that all appreciated by ten times in the space of five years. The profit that he personally derived from his position as *"zhuang"* came to several billion RMB. Meanwhile, the three companies under his banner did rather poorly. Net profits altogether came to only some RMB 240 million, far below the miraculous results that one might have expected given the price of the shares. In

One of the 'Ten Great Engineering Projects' in the western part of China successfully cut off the flow of water at Zipingpu, to create a catchment basin. The Wenchuan earthquake of May 12, 2008, occurred in this region of Sichuan.

order to keep the share prices up, he constantly engaged in capital-market activity by either buying other companies or declaring that he was doing so. He would use the combined earnings to puff up corporate results, and so stabilize and lift shares. At the same time, this gentleman also founded and controlled several trust-finance institutions, and was active in banks, securities, financial leasing, insurance, and funds, so that, through various legal and also illegal methods he developed the business of being in fiduciary control of other people's money. Operating in "grey areas" which the laws had not yet addressed with any specificity, and using irregular practices that were definitely illegal, allowed this person to evolve into a frightening and dangerous financial monster. The costs of operating his enterprise amounted to RMB 1 billion every year, spent on maintaining and manipulating share-prices. In addition, interest charges on financing of share purchases required another RMB 3 billion. This is to say, RMB 4 billion in capital was necessary every year to guarantee normal operations. The sum was high enough to guarantee that the operations of this *zhuang-jia* would eventually come tumbling down.

The importance of a responsible media in developing a healthy stock market cannot be over-emphasized. The magazine *Caijing*, based in Beijing, has done more than any other form of

media in China to assure the necessary transparency. In October of 2000, *Caijing* published a cover story about "the murky screen behind which funds operate," which pierced one nice myth about the stock markets that was going around. Before this, fund companies were felt to be worthy of trust, unlike the avaricious *zhuang-jia*. They relied on professional management and scientific approaches. Since 1998, every group of funds that came to market carried the support of regulatory officials and of the public at large. These funds were seen as importing Western experience, assimilating the experience of mature markets. They were important in the development of institutional investors. In the end, however, people discovered that funds were not the angels they were meant to be. Like *zhuang-jia*, they employed irregular practices, including illegal manipulative behavior. The

Upper: Looking from Shanghai's Bund across the Whampoa River to Lujiazui in Pudong. Pudong means East of the Pu, 'Pu' referring to the Huangpu river or Whampoa in English. To a degree, in the minds of some Chinese the height of Pudong represents the elevated status of China. Photographed in February 2008.

Lower left: A young person plays volleyball before some old buildings in Shanghai. Pudong's Oriental Pearl Tower is in the background, built in 2004.

Lower right: Swimmers on the Huangpu River.

Caijing article stirred up quite some waves in what had been a fairly tranquil part of the sea.

Fund companies were indignant at the charges. Just as the rebuttals were coming thick and fast, a seventy-year-old economist named Wu Jinglian stood forth to address the subject in an interview on television. He agreed with people who compared the markets to gambling dens, but went further. He said, "Some foreigners say that the Chinese stock market is like a gambling den, highly irregular in its operations. But gambling dens have their rules. For example, you are not allowed to see other people's cards. In our stock markets, privileged people are allowed to see other people's cards. They can commit fraud with impunity, they can engage in deceit and trickery. They can and do manipulate share prices." After delivering an attack on both *zhuang-jia* and funds, Wu Jinglian turned to the larger issue of the purpose and "positioning" of China's capital markets. He said, "We cannot turn the stock market into a place for rent-seeking. Authorities have positioned the stock market as being a financing service for State-owned enterprises. They have skewed the market by making it into a tool for getting funds on behalf of these enterprises. Any company that is granted the right to list on the market is able to derive its working capital out of excessively high-priced share distributions. The money comes from the hands of those who buy the shares, not from normal business operations. This has turned the entire stock market into a huge rent-seeking fair in which State-owned enterprises go shopping for breakfast. We must reject a policy that allows this, and reject a way of doing things that says, 'the government leaves it up to the market, and enterprises rake in the money.'"

This gentleman, humble, mild, and likeable, was later called the "conscience of Chinese economics" because of his courage in saying these things.

Stock market problems revealed the youth and immaturity of China's capital markets. Overall, however, the market also enabled a more vibrant economy and allowed entrepreneurs to exercise their creativity. These entrepreneurs were fueled in part by overseas examples.

foreign enterprises

foreign products

WTO

Chinese Market

China's entry into the WTO represented an opportunity both to China and to the world.

On September 27, 1999, *Fortune* had its annual meeting in Shanghai. Three hundred multinational company executives attended, among whom sixty or more were CEOs from Fortune 500 companies. A UPI reporter wrote, "It felt like being at the Super Bowl, the time, the place, the excitement, were all there, and people were witnessing a classic competition." In contrast to the matter-of-fact attitudes of foreign CEOs, some two hundred Chinese entrepreneurs who were there were hyper-excited. They yearned to receive the "holy scripture" from world-class entrepreneurs. Many people later regarded this event as a symbolic marker in the ascent of China.

Another piece of good news came on November 15, 1999, when a truly global "entry ticket" was finally extended to China. On this day, China and America formally came to an agreement that allowed America to express its support for China's entry into the WTO.

The negotiations toward this end had hit a stalemate in May 1991, for on May 8, American guided missiles bombed the Chinese embassy in Belgrade, and three journalists were killed. University students in Beijing took to the streets, where they lit candles and held a silent vigil for the dead before the American Embassy. As representative of America,

College students demonstrating against the NATO guided missiles that hit the Chinese Embassy in Belgrade.

certain multinational companies braced for demonstrations. McDonald's closed its doors for a day; the IBM building had broken windows from hurled stones; Microsoft's CEO for the greater China region told employees in an email, "The company can shut its doors if need be, and employees are allowed to go home to avoid any trouble." Students are marvelously flexible, however, for at the Computer Department at Peking University, for example, they hung out a banner saying, "Embargo American goods… except for the computers." Many other students spent the daytime demonstrating, then went home at night to study for their TOEFL exams in order to go to America. While the sentiment against America was proceeding, Japan and America announced a Japanese-American Defense Cooperation Agreement, in the hypothetical event of mutual enemies in the Asian region.

The crisis eventually passed, and Sino-American WTO negotiations reached a successful conclusion at the end of 1999. For one hundred years, Chinese had hoped to enter the global family as a positive and equal member. In the very last year of the twentieth century, the country was finally able to gain an entry ticket to the game.

China enters the final rounds of the World Cup after it's national team defeated Oman in Shenyang in 2001.

Stride on over the Rainbow

At 10 pm on July 13, 2001, all Chinese people drew a collective sigh of relief. People had been waiting for this moment for four long years. When they saw Juan Antonio Samaranch, President of the Olympic Commission, open a sealed envelope and say one word with vigor, "Beijing," firecrackers and explosions of joy went off throughout the country. From that moment all the way up to 2008, the Olympics were to be the engine driving the Chinese economy and also a major psychological force behind an economic boom.

Winning the bid for the Olympics gave China a chance to show itself to the world, but even more importantly brought a tremendous boost to the economy.

More good news was to follow. The saying went around, "2001 is China's year." On October 7, the Chinese men's soccer team played at Shenyang Liaoning, and beat Oman 1:0, thereby enabling the Chinese team to enter the final rounds of the World Cup and to realize a dream the Chinese had wanted for years, to "break out of Asia and stride into

The WTO talks achieved a breakthrough in 2001 at Doha, Qatar. On the right is China's Minister of Foreign Trade and Economic Cooperation, Shi Guangsheng.

Soccer fans kissed before the match between China and Brazil during the 2002 FIFA World Cup.

the world." On November 10, the WTO held a Ministerial-level meeting in Dakar, and reviewed and passed a motion to allow China to join the World Trade Organization.

The economic significance of China's joining WTO had become apparent several years earlier, and been factored into Chinese strategic policy. This began in 1998 with the "State out, People in" policy. The reorganization and ensuing activities of State-owned capital groups were, without exception, choreographed to coincide with the WTO timetable for opening up markets. The result was that large State-owned enterprises began to exhibit their highest profit levels since the 1990s.

Blood transfusions into large State-owned enterprises, and their general resuscitation, were manifested in three distinct ways. First was the way in which Chinese companies were listed on overseas exchanges. The successful listing in either New York or Hong Kong of China Telecom, China Unicom, China Petroleum and so on were examples. That conservative State-owned organizations were now

"charging overseas" was a function not only of getting financing, but of a tremendous determination to undertake transformational change. Second was a strengthening of competition in many fields, with the divesting of what had formerly been huge monopolies. China Telecom was divided into five parts, Sino Petroleum and Sinopec were separated from each other, Air China was reorganized, China National Nonferrous Metals was dispersed in various regions, China's five large military-industrial groups were divided into ten. Basically all of the old-brand State-owned enterprises underwent some kind of dismembering. Third was that certain entrepreneurs of Chinese companies began to show their merits and to be recognized as real agents for change. People who had been low-key but successful were now pushed to the top of the wave, and their potential as world-class entrepreneurs was reinforced.

Multinational companies that had been entrenched in China for many years now were quick to modify their own strategies in the new post-WTO business environment. Companies that previously had no alternative but to form joint ventures now began to divest themselves of their Chinese partners and to set up solely-invested companies.

For many years, any foreign-invested factory in China had to have a local partner with whom it formed a joint venture.

The 9th APEC leader's conference was held in Shanghai. Leaders donned Tang-style clothes for this group photograph.

Foreign banks in the Lujiazui finance and trade zone of Pudong, Shanghai. China has become a mecca for financial investors.

In each region in which Coca-Cola or PepsiCo had a bottling factory, for example, the companies had to form a joint venture with the State-operated cereal, oils, and foodstuffs company (COFCO). P&G was similarly told that its partners were going to be the personal-care chemical plants. After China entered the WTO, however, such restrictions were eliminated. Multinationals that already had joint ventures in China went through all kinds of measures to disengage from the Chinese investor and become a solely-invested entity. Matsushita, for example, declared to the media, "All of the fifty joint venture companies that Matsushita has in China are going to be turned into solely invested companies." Motorola, which manufactured cell phones in China, came to the same conclusion. Its board of directors decided that within the next five years it would increase its investment in China to USD 10 billion. The board of directors had determined that "becoming solely invested is a natural decision since China entered the World Trade Organization." After the carbonated beverages market was opened, Coca-Cola and PepsiCo, the two giants, began determined moves in the direction of sole investments, and PepsiCo was even willing to take up litigation against its previous China-side partner.

At the same time, multinationals began to enter into fields

that could be described as more "monopolistic" and less "competitive." In the early and middle periods of reform and opening up, the great majority of multinationals that came into China were in completely competitive market arenas. The ones that achieved the greatest success were Coca-Cola, producing beverages, P&G, producing shampoo, and Japanese companies, producing home electronics. As Chinese companies moved into these consumer areas, multinationals found it increasingly hard to compete, unless their Chinese competitors made some fatal mistake. After 2001, multinationals began to enter natural-resource industries since, for the first time, they were allowed to invest in cooperative ventures in these areas. In general, they moved out of businesses in which they were in head-on competition with people-operated enterprises, and they moved in the direction of industries that excluded people-operated enterprises. For example, GE shifted its investment focus from household items to things incorporating more technology such as medical diagnostic equipment, gas turbines, wind turbines, hydro-electric power equipment, airplane engines, electric transmission and so on. Such investments promised excellent returns in China and most were in areas where people-operated capital was forbidden to enter.

Multinationals also briskly entered the field of financial investments. The opening of China's financial markets was given a timetable after WTO entry, and all large financial institutions now increased their China operations. By 2001, HSBC, Citibank, AIG Private Bank, Standard Chartered and other such banks had moved their regional headquarters from Singapore or Hong Kong to Shanghai. Some that had quietly set up organizations earlier now began to float to the light of day. According to the *Economic Observer*, many years earlier, Morgan Stanley had set up a venture with the China Construction Bank and others called CICC, the China International Capital Corporation, the "only and the most outstanding joint venture investment bank in China." Morgan Stanley held 35% of shares. In October of 2001, for the first time China permitted foreign-investment to join in the disposition of nonperforming loans. At the first auction for these bundled loans, Morgan

Upper: A grade school in an old revolutionary base in the countryside. There has been no fundamental change in thirty years in the disgracefully bad elementary education in poor mountainous areas.

Middle left: A postman goes up and around rugged terrain to deliver the mail. Photographed in August 2001.

Middle right: Performing for customers in a restaurant. The market for high-brow culture was depressed when this photograph was taken in 2000, so that actresses had to rely on this kind of job to make ends meet.

Lower left: Peddlers who relied on the railroad traffic for their living, selling food to passengers in April 2002.

Lower right: Workers' dormitory in Panyu, Guangdong Province, September 2002.

A reform to 'clarify and demarcate ownership of assets' began in 1998. This made trillionaires out of some people, but also led to the downfall of some formerly 'star' enterprises. This photograph shows Li Jingwei, founder of the health beverages company Jianlibao, sitting in one corner at a meeting. His enterprise was hastily sold although the equivalent price that he had offered was rejected. This photograph has been called one of the saddest in the history of contemporary entrepreneurs.

Stanley, as a sole investor, was able to purchase packaged assets worth an estimated RMB 10.8 billion. The assets were distributed throughout eighteen of China's provinces and cities, and included 254 companies and factories in the fields of real estate, textiles, metallurgy, pharmaceuticals and other industries. Most were previously assets of State-owned enterprises. Clearly, these non-performing assets were "surplus value" resulting from the strategic policy of "State out, People in."

While multinational capital continued to penetrate all corners of China, and State-owned capital made a strong comeback through reorganization, a Third Force, namely people-operated capital, was vigorously contending for a place in the sun.

Finance had been a monopoly in China, reserved for State-owned banks. Any privately operated enterprise was dreaming if it thought it could get a piece of that particular cake. Now, however, a people-operated enterprise became the largest shareholder of a bank called the China Minsheng Bank, holding 7.98%

of its shares. This bank was small, but represented an experi-
mental-type commercial bank that had clearly delineated ownership. Other areas also opened up to what in the West would
be called private enterprise. One Chinese entrepreneur who had
returned from overseas astutely found a space between the two
huge giants in China's telecommunications industry. Technology that had been discarded abroad became his weapon. The
company he founded, UT Starcom, traded at a level that gave
his company a market capitalization of around USD 26 billion.
The grassroots-born Zhejiang entrepreneur Li Shufu, after strug-
gling for close to ten years, was able to get the first government
license for a people-operated auto-manufacturing business. No
matter whether he was successful or not, this private enterprise
called Geely now had the chance to compete in the international
arena. This license to Li Shufu was soon interpreted as opening up a major industry in China after the country's entry into
WTO.

China's entry into the WTO was an exciting and promising
development for almost everyone. The organization seemed
like a beautiful rainbow, an inviting gateway, and once China
finally stepped through that gateway the entire country drew
a tremendous sigh of relief. Others, however, were noting developments in China with some alarm. Predicting China's future had become a favored topic of international circles. Japan
issued a White Paper in which it was noted that China had
already become "factory to the world," that "Made in China"
was ubiquitous and the country had number one market share
in color TVs, washing machines, refrigerators, air condition-
ing, microwaves, motorcycles, and many other products. The
"China Threat" had arrived.

Still others were less optimistic than China about the benefits
of entering the WTO. An overseas-Chinese American lawyer
named Gordon G. Chang predicted "The Coming Collapse of
China" in a book of that title. This declared that China's prosperity was a chimera, that the country would receive a setback
after entering WTO due to increased competition. Chang believed that China's existing political and economic system could
persevere for another five years at most and then would be

Miners work for years in the world's most dangerous and most difficult conditions, some one-thousand meters underground. A tremendous number of small mines are worked by these men, leading to increasing numbers of mining accidents and heightened public concern for safety.

faced with massive problems. Similarly, Salomon Smith Barney (now under Citigroup) predicted that, after the first five years of China's entry into WTO, China would see 40 million unemployed, and that the severe employment pressure would sooner or later lead to the fall of the government.

China's economic growth appeared to follow its own internal logic, however, erratic as that might seem to outsiders. The above forecasts have not been realized to date and both overly pessimistic and optimistic views appear unfounded. As the late, eminent economist, John Kenneth Galbraith, said in a talk on Sino-American relations, "Many of our predictions about China are merely guesses."

The coal mining industry in China is facing depletion after decades of exploitation. Like their fathers before them, young coal miners are leaving home to try to make a living elsewhere.

Yao Ming, China's most famous basketball star, is also described as China's most expensive export to America.

The China Threat

The term "Made in China" began to get heightened attention in the global media in around 2002, as the world began to feel the existence and the power of China.

In 2002, China exported its single most expensive commodity, a basketball player named Yao Ming. Yao Ming is 2.26 meters tall. People have calculated that if he stays in the NBA until he is 38 years old, his salary will be between USD 270 and 290 million, not including the income he gets from sponsoring products. This sum is roughly equal to China's exporting 1.02 million tons of rice or 460,000 tons of steel, 2.39 million color television sets or 6.3 million bicycles, 980,000 tons of crude oil or 64.89 million meters of silk. It is quite true that "Made in China" is ubiquitous, and part of the reason is Wal-Mart's. The New York Times journalist Thomas Friedman calculated that,

"If Wal-Mart were a country, it would be China's eighth largest trading partner, and sixth largest in terms of taking in China exports." By the beginning of 2002, Wal-Mart's purchases in China came to USD 12 billion, roughly the same as the total trade volume between China and Russia. In 2002, Wal-Mart moved its Asian purchasing center from Hong Kong to the Lu-ohu district of Shenzhen.

"Made in China" had already become an unassailable fact of life in the late 1990s as "cheap but well-made" Chinese products spread around the globe. The Chinese soccer team did not win at the 2002 Korea-Japan FIFA World Cup, but Chinese products did. Yangzhou in Jiangsu Province made 300,000 World Cup good-luck items, Yiwu in Zhejiang produced 2,250,000 soccer-fan flags. Fujian factories supplied several million other soccer items. Any Chinese traveling to another country and wanting to buy a souvenir soon discovered that anything that could be purchased had been made in China.

The reason, as astute people have noted, is that "Made in China" takes advantage of very cheap labor. The experience of the company Galanz is a prime example. Based in Guangdong, Galanz is the world's largest manufacturer of microwave ovens. In 2002, its factories produced more than 12 million microwaves, more than one-third of total world production. The most important advanced component of a microwave is its pressure-changing device. Japan produces this for a cost of USD 20; European and American companies make it for more than USD 30. Galanz approached American companies, knowing that they were facing stiff competition from Japanese makers. It said, "Let us make the devices and we will charge you USD 8 at current American production quantities." Americans were happy to send their production lines on over to China. Since wages of Galanz factory workers are extremely low, and since three shifts operate twenty-four hours a day, Galanz factories can produce all of America's production in just two days of each week. The rest of the time is like having a free lunch in terms of using the production line for other markets. Galanz then went to Japan to negotiate, saying, "We will sell you each piece for USD 5, if you send your production lines over and

Starting in 1998, Chinese products began to conquer world markets as a result of China's low-cost advantage. At the same time, 'Made in China' provoked anti-dumping responses from many countries.

lease them to us." This process was repeated elsewhere and the production lines of several countries converged on Guangdong. Due to its cheap labor costs, Galanz became the world's factory for microwaves, the dragon-head, the number one.

Many have doubts about the sustainability of the "Made-in-China" formula, but others recognize that "Made in China" is just the prelude to China's ascent. The bigger picture includes a well-rounded economy that functions in areas beyond simple manufacturing. The foundations for this kind of economy were put in place by Zhu Rongji. From 1991, when he was appointed Vice Premier directly in charge of China's economy, until 1998, when he formally assumed the responsibilities of premier, Zhu Rongji used both his professional talents and his native instincts to reform China's economy in a fundamental way. During his tenure, macro-economic policies followed what was called the "three-eight rule" (the 38th parallel). Inflation was

Workers demanding that back pay be paid up. On July 10, 2004, workers who had been building a road approached the construction company gates and asked for their pay. Their wages were already seven or eight years in arrears. The entity responsible for paying the money turned out to be the local government.

The rise of China's athletic prowess has been taken as a symbol of national power. This photo shows China's female Table Tennis players took the first three places at the Sydney Olympic Games in 2000. The third-place winner was Chen Jing, representing Chinese Taipei in the competition.

to be kept under 3%, and GDP growth was to be kept over 8%. In a turbulent period, when one century rolled into the next, it was this sustained, high-speed growth that allowed China to maintain a prosperous outlook. As Chinese began to say to the rest of the world, "the view is excellent from this side."

At the turn of the century, new forms began growing into the skeleton of old structures in China. Two brief vignettes exemplify this process. In Shanghai, a Chinese businessman moved two thousand people out of their old homes but kept the homes intact and made them into a kind of upscale walking district. He called it "Xintiandi," or "New Heaven and Earth." As evening falls, the most fashionable young people in Shanghai can be seen strolling along its narrow streets and alleys, stopping

in at swank bars, restaurants, art galleries. Old Shanghai tunes can be heard wafting from elegant stores; Chinese rub shoulders in this place with young people from all over the world. It represents a microcosm of a new future. Very rarely do people notice that in the southeastern corner of Xintiandi is an old two-story

A toy factory in Yangzhou, China, with workers on the production line.

Left: Xintiandi, located near Huaihai Road in Shanghai, is a sole remaining vestige of the old city. As dusk falls, young people from all over the world stroll here, listening to the sweet strains of the music of the old Shanghai, enjoying the shops and restaurants in narrow old alleys, called '*long*' in Shanghainese. Blond-haired, blue-eyed westerners rub shoulders with fashionable young Chinese.

Right: '798' was originally a munitions factory, built in the 1950s in Beijing and given a numeral since it belonged to the military. In 2002, some young people started a kind of artist's community here, bringing an old district to life again. It has become a very trendy place in Beijing.

house that has been preserved intact. Eighty years ago, thirteen young people met in this house to announce the formation of the Communist Party of China.

Another example is the renovation of a district in Beijing. A young woman involved in cultural pursuits discovered that a huge factory district in the northeast corner of the city was neglected and up for rent. Its buildings had housed a munitions factory from the 1950s and due to its military nature it was given the rather mysterious-sounding name of "798." The lady rented one of the factory buildings for an extremely cheap price and created a workshop for her own artistic endeavors, while an American friend rented another space for his website design studio. Soon, other creative people were moving into other parts of the complex and the "798 artists group" snowballed. A creative and dynamic cultural phenomenon now exists in what used to be a weapons factory.

As cultural life blossomed in the late 1990s and the early part of the twenty-first century, a new willingness to look frankly at China's problems also appeared. People began to use a kind of black humor to describe the phenomenon of China's nouveau riche, in particular. These people were widely believed to have gained their wealth through illegal means. A public opinion poll done by the Renmin University of China indicated that 60% of those polled felt this way. A movie called *Big Wrists*, meaning a knack for making deals, became an explosive hit among State-produced movies in 2002. This comedy ridiculed people in what were called "explosive wealth" circles. This "explosive wealth" is increasingly being scrutinized. When the State Administration

The Englishman Rupert Hoogewerf has been ranking China's wealthiest people since 1999. His annual list creates movie-star fame for the wealthy, but also brings them the negative consequences of exposure.

of Taxation made public the top fifty privately-managed enterprises that were paying the most in taxes in China, this became an excellent resource for comparative purposes. Someone took that list and compared it to the top fifty names of Chinese companies on the Fortune 500 list. Only four of the names corresponded.

At around the same time, *Time* magazine published a special report on China about "The Pitiful Super-rich." The author described the lifestyle of China's wealthy, and it named names. "These people build luxurious offices that copy the inside of the Oval Office in the White House, they try to replicate Rockefeller's estate in their second homes, yet in these homes, on the outskirts of cities, they hardly dare to turn on the fancy chandeliers, for fear that poor neighbors will be attracted and come over the gate. Their wives tolerate the fact that their husbands take numerous lovers. The wives comfort themselves with buying luxury items, burning incense at temples, and having more babies to pass the time." The article went on to describe an impoverished sort of mindless indulgence. This article was translated and soon made its way to the internet in China, where it was passed around, bringing considerable trouble to the interviewees.

PART FIVE

Responsibility and Reason
2003–2008

SARS, Housing Bubbles, Electricity Panics

Zhu Rongji gave his final working report to the government on March 5, 2003, together with formal notice of his retirement. Sixty-one-year-old Wen Jiabao succeeded him as Premier. On the very next day, news broke out in Beijing that an "uncommon" or acute epidemic had invaded China, with journalists reporting it as a kind of "avenging spirit" called SARS.

SARS is a highly contagious inflammation of the lungs that can lead to sudden death. The moment a person suspected of having it is detected, he must be quarantined. While scientists were still trying to figure out what it was, SARS was spreading rapidly through China. From Guangdong Province it spread to Hong Kong, Shanghai, and Beijing, and soon deaths were being reported almost daily. By April 28, confirmed cases in Beijing alone totaled 1,199 people, while suspected cases added 1,275 people. Fifty-nine in Beijing were already dead. In short order, SARS became the number one issue facing the country. For the next six months, daily life and business operations in China were totally disrupted. Enterprises faced each day with a kind of terror.

SARS is called *"fei-dian"* in Chinese, which means "atypical." The abbreviation was appropriate to the sudden appearance and frightening nature of the disease. The panic lasted until June 24, when the World Health Organization announced it was lifting its Travel Advisory to Beijing.

Left: The SARS epidemic of 2003 put China through a test. This photo shows a third-year middle school student, mask over her mouth but face wreathed in smiles, sitting in a classroom of the #171 Middle School in Beijing's eastern district on May 22, 2003.

Right: Street scene during the SARS period.

China's economic growth for the year 2003 was not in fact highly affected by the disruption of SARS. The first two quarters were impacted, with growth slipping down to 6.7%, but by the third quarter the rate had quickly revived and, by the end of the year, GDP growth rate reached 9.1%. Not only was this higher than the year before, but it was highest since 1997. The hardest hit businesses were tourism, air travel, restaurants, entertainment and other such services. Unexpected business opportunities landed in the lap of some sectors, including pharmaceuticals, food, textiles, and telecommunications. In fact, China's resilience in the wake of "SARS" was bittersweet. On the one hand, it reflected the internal strength of China's economy; on the other, it showed the beginnings of an overheated economy.

"Made in China" continued to march out into the world. According to an American consulting company, A. T. Kearney, "Made in China" dominated in more than one hundred fields worldwide. These included containers, electronics, and electronic toys: China produced 90% of containers in the world, 80% of DVD players, 75% of toys, 70% of gifts, 65% of athletic equipment, 60% of bicycles, 50% of microwave ovens, 30% of color televisions and refrigerators, and the list went on.

An explosive real estate market kept pace with foreign trade. "Buying consortiums" helped stoke the fever. People would see "Wenzhou buying groups" near newly built buildings in cities all along China's coast. They went around with little wooden placards announcing their presence, wanting to buy apartments or whole buildings, as casual as if they were simply out there buying vegetables. In fact, they wanted to buy all real estate in sight.

A market in Beijing under the famous White Pagoda.

An article in the Shanghai *Oriental Morning Post* explored this phenomenon. It noted that the money came from normal Wenzhou people, investors whose money had been pooled in order to speculate in real estate. It said, "Wenzhou people are speculating throughout the country on buildings, using RMB 10 million at a shot. An army of around 80,000 Wenzhou people are out there purchasing buildings. Over 90% of these purchases are being bought to flip over for quick return. Conservative estimates are that more than 70,000 of these 80,000 people are simply speculating. The principals in the business are white-collar managers and relatives of government officials. At a return of 15%, an investment of RMB 100 trillion can make RMB 15 billion in a year, which is a pretty fast way to make money. Real estate speculation is now the primary business of Wenzhou." The term the article used in Chinese for the activity of Wenzhou buyers is "*chao*," which means the same as "stir-fry:" quick in, quick out.

Wherever Wenzhou people went, housing prices rose sharply. When the general price level of any given city had risen to a certain degree, they would stage an orderly exit and move on. Like a swarm of locusts, they would blanket the next city.

As urbanization spread across China, hordes of these housing buyers came right after them. Supply could not meet demand in most cities, so along with the rise in prices came a kind of panic buying. This was the opportunity in a thousand years for the people building the housing. Real estate was where the explosive profits were to be made, just as it had been in Japan, Hong Kong and Taiwan in the 1970s. A 2003 edition of *Forbes* magazine noted, "People have been amazed to see that forty of the top one hundred wealthiest people on China's mainland are in real estate. Six of the top ten are in real estate. No wonder there is a saying in China these days, 'Once a person gets a taste for doing real estate, he's addicted. He won't be willing to do any other business ever again.'"

"Made in China" and the real estate craze created an economic structure that was irrational, not the product of organic growth. Yes, a prosperous period had come again, but together

Beijing City Planning Museum. A visitor looking at the city map.

Notice of electricity stoppage at a shopping mall. Energy shortages have plagued the Chinese economy for a long time.

with it came a ferocious rise in prices of all raw materials and resources.

The "electricity panic" was the epitome of this process. An electricity shortage darkened provinces and cities across China after the summer of 2003. The largest consumers of electricity, including Shanghai, Guangdong, Jiangsu, Zhejiang, and even coal-rich Shanxi, all began to experience blackouts as electricity was cut. In order to deal with the crisis, strange announcements were issued about "open two shut down one," and "open five shut down two," and so on. There were even "open three shut down four" electricity-use plans, which meant that an enterprise could stay open and use electricity for only three out of seven days in a week. For the other four, it shut down. Large enterprises with an allocation under the "Plan" were exempt. Other enterprises, especially in places like Zhejiang and Jiangsu where small and medium-sized operations were the rule, were much harder hit. This situation had not been seen since 1978. Some markets in towns and cities carried on in the evening with candles, including the Bund in Shanghai.

Hit by the "electricity panic," the prices of all kinds of raw materials and resources that were already in short supply began to rise. Cement and steel prices went up at the rate of three price increases per month. Steel producers were happy.

Liu Chuanzhi, founder of China's largest computer company, Lenovo, transfers his duties as President to a man twenty years his junior, Yang Yuanqing. Chinese entrepreneurs complete their first 'succession.'

In the Yangtze River Delta region, a saying went around about the "Five ones." "It takes an investment of ten million RMB to produce one ton of steel. Producing one million tons takes one year, and in one year you get back your full investment."

In order to satisfy this runaway domestic demand, China's large State-owned resource companies began to scour the world for resources. They covered the globe, looking for oil, metals, natural gas. All international markets began to express alarm: "The starving tiger of China is upon us!" Clever international buyers immediately formed alliances and, as a group put up the price. Chinese soon found that, "whatever you want to buy gets expensive, and whatever you want to sell gets cheap." News of the discovery of a large oil field in the Bohai Bay was comforting to Premier Wen Jiabao.

The tremendous economic surge aroused State-owned enterprises and privately-owned

A woman worker on the assembly line.

Construction worker at a construction site.

enterprises, particularly in the area of heavy chemicals due to the huge profits. In the severe macro-economic adjustments that were to follow, many of the privately-owned enterprises had to close. In 2002, total investment in the steel industry in China was RMB 71 billion, a rise of 45.9% over the previous year. In 2003, this figure rose to RMB 132.9 billion, a rise of 96%. Other industries rose in sync: investment in electroplated aluminum rose 92.9%, in cement 121.9%. These phenomenal increases in investment in natural resources and the concurrent over-heating of the economy eventually came to the attention of policy makers. At the end of 2003, they began to blow the whistle.

While a "thunderclap" of macro-economic adjustments hit the country, in the form of tightened interest rates, restrictions on bank loans and other measures, authorities also wielded their knife on a real estate market that was causing howls of alarm from the public. A rapid string of edicts was issued to address the situation. From March to May of 2004, the State Council tightened the issuing of currency and the size of loans, increased controls on land use, put a stop to or tried to put a stop to the encroachments on agricultural land, "reorganized" funded projects that either were under way or had just been built, and strengthened "credit risk management" which means made it harder to get money. At the same time, all large

Liu Xiang, the 110-meter sprinter, took the championship at the 2004 Olympics. He and Yao Ming are China's two most famous athletes.

papers in China began discussing the real estate overheating, and suddenly this industry became a "political problem." People who had been engaged in it were subject to much greater scrutiny and some were prosecuted.

All these actions changed the earnings expectations of investors as well as the price expectations of consumers when they purchased housing. More importantly, they changed the government's ideas about supporting real estate development as a tool in macro-economic policy. This led directly to a swift contraction in building-market deals. Winter suddenly

Twenty years after the start of reform and opening up, people were no longer shocked and amazed by modern art.

descended upon the real estate industry.

As tightening measures began to take effect, the stock markets responded by falling as well. By the end of 2004, the Shanghai Exchange index and the Shenzhen Exchange index had fallen by 15.4% and 16.6% respectively, to end at 1266.5 and 315.81. This was their lowest since the year 2000.

International observers were at a loss to understand the storm of macro-economic measures that occurred in China between the spring and summer of 2004. *New York Times* columnist Thomas Friedman wrote, "These days, leaders in America, Europe, Japan and the key countries in Asia pray to the Chinese economy before going to bed at night. The world has gradually become hostage to China's cheap labor, its need for raw materials, and foreign investment, and its tremendous capital power. When the China bubble bursts, all kinds of bubbles around the world will go with it." At the end of May, the Korean government held a series of emergency meetings to analyze the impact of China's "braking" policies on Korea. Even the normally cautious Chairman of the Federal Reserve, Alan Greenspan, openly expressed his concern. In a speech to the House of Representatives of Congress, he said, "If China runs into problems, it will have a direct effect on the Japanese and Southeast Asian economies, but it will also have an indirect effect on us."

Once more, China's economic performance made scholars around the world adjust the spectacles on their noses. In the third quarter of 2004, the Asian Development Bank forecast that the growth rate in China's GDP would fall to 8.3%, while China's Ministry of Commerce was even more conservative and put it at 7.5%. In the end, China's State Statistical Bureau showed that the growth rate of GDP in 2004 was 10.1%, the fastest growth rate in any year since 1996. Investment in fixed assets in the country was RMB 7 trillion, an increase of 25.8% over the previous year. Exports exceeded USD 1 trillion. All indicators showed that the Chinese economy was still on a fast-track. People later judged the macro-economic measures to be more of a light tap on the brakes than a real braking.

The Long March 2F carrier rocket took the Shenzhou #6 spacecraft into the heavens at 9 o'clock sharp on October 12, 2005. Photographed at the Satellite Launch Center in Jiuquan, China.

Trade Frictions

October 12, 2005, was another historic day for China. Two Chinese astronauts flew into space on the Chinese-made Shenzhou #6 spacecraft. The word *"shenzhou"* signifies a land of the gods, and is a traditional way of referring to the motherland. Two years earlier, on October 12, China's first astronaut rode into space on the Shenzhou #5, realizing a millennial dream of Chinese people to fly through the skies.

Ascending into the stratosphere with this space ship was China's economic clout. One day in 2005, a journalist living in Baton Rouge decided to spend a year without using anything "Made in China." She first threw out her son's shoes. She went to the local European discount shoe store to buy a new non-Chinese pair, but found that the place had closed since business was so bad.

The first Chinese astronaut that flied into space, Yang Li-wei.

Instead a toy store occupied the space, and everything in the toy store was made in China. Household utensils were another problem. When hers broke she took them to be repaired, but what appeared to be "Made in U.S.A." were in fact full of spare parts produced in China. From mousetraps to lanterns to birthday candles to firecrackers, it was as hard to find anything not made in China as it was to go to heaven. She wrote her experience into a book, called *A Year without "Made in China."* Her conclusion was that she and her family had to compromise with reality, since otherwise the price was too great.

Nothing could speak more clearly than this woman's experience. Cheap prices were the sole weapon in the "Made-in-China" arsenal, and the cheap prices were making it hard for the rest of the world to compete. As a result, the manufacturing industries of all countries were faced with a severe challenge. The other side to China's success in exporting was that trade frictions rose and China soon became the focus of anti-dumping cases at the WTO. Of every seven anti-dumping and trade emergency cases, one was aimed at China.

Back in June of 2002, the European Union had begun an anti-dumping case against the Wenzhou region of China with regard to cigarette lighters. This became Case Number One in Anti-Dumping, after China's entry into the WTO. At the time, several hundred companies in Wenzhou were producing 90% of the world's metal-sheathed lighters, and the cost of production was one-tenth what it cost in Japan. In its defense, Wenzhou enterprises said that the main reason China prices were cheaper was that their cost of labor was cheaper. The annual income of Wenzhou workers was one-twentieth that of European workers. Their argument was, "Chinese enterprises do not engage in loss-making business." This defense was successful in the end, and the European Union withdrew the case. Wenzhou tradespeople, famous throughout China for their cheap and shoddy goods, now became the country's heroes. Even today, they are applauded for this victory.

The victory of the "Defensive War for cigarette-lighters" did not slow down an ongoing wave of anti-dumping cases, however. On September 16, 2004, a demonstration against Wenzhou shoes erupted in Elche, Spain. Several hundred

Spanish shoe-makers came to docks where Chinese goods were being offloaded and destroyed sixteen containers full of Wenzhou shoes worth an estimated USD 1 million. One week later, another demonstration erupted in Elche where several thousand people marched in the street, a sizeable percentage of the town's population of 200,000. The same emotions were being aroused in Italy. According to statistics of the Italian Shoe Manufacturing Industry Federation, more than 250 million pairs of Chinese shoes had been imported into Italy in the past two years, a figure that for the first time exceeded the number of shoes exported. This was humiliating to a country that prided itself on its shoe-manufacturing industry. The European Union instituted a special label called "Not Made in China" after this, in order to comfort local manufacturers.

Chinese officials and experts tried to explain this uncomfortable situation from China's standpoint, and to ameliorate the friction. In May of 2005, the Minister of China's Ministry of Commerce, Bo Xilai, attended a forum in Paris called, "Sino-French small and medium-sized industry cooperation forum." When he was asked his attitude about Chinese textile dumping, the seasoned negotiator replied, "Perhaps you have not done the calculations, but China must sell 800 million shirts before it can import one Airbus 380 aircraft." A key fact relevant

The 23rd summer Olympics held in Los Angeles in 1984. Li Ning, dubbed 'Prince of Gymnasts,' is representing China.

Founded by the former Olympic champion gymnast, the company Li-Ning ranks fourth among general sports companies, after Nike, Adidas, and Puma. Li Ning, Chairman, is photographed here on March 21, 2007.

The 2008 Olympics filled the Chinese people with hope and confidence.

to Bo Xilai's statement is that, in the past two years, China had purchased thirty passenger planes, among which five were the expensive French Airbus 380.

On June 6, 2005, the Shanghai index fell to 998.22, and stayed there, the first time it had stayed below the holding line of 1000 in eight years. Much had been made of this "thousand-point benchmark" and people who had said the market couldn't fall below that mark now began to cry as they saw the numbers move south. Paradoxically, since the markets had fallen to a point where they could fall no further, it was an excellent time to start implementing new reforms. Low share prices were what finally enabled a resolution of ownership issues in a number of State-owned enterprises. The reform was known as "division of share ownership."

As noted above, for a long time China had maintained two classes of shares, those that could be traded and those that could not. The legal rights of shareholders who held the traded shares were trampled upon by the system, however, since they were in a minority. Small and medium shareholders were particularly vulnerable. The system was custom-made to incubate all the evils of the *"zhuang-jia"* phenomenon, the manipulative banker in a gambling game. For ten whole years, this phenomenon had been recognized and vigorously denounced

by experts. The benefits of the dual-share system were so substantial to certain interest groups, however, that all proposals to change it were blocked. When the detrimental effect of the system began to influence the entire stock market, however, negatively impacting special interest groups as well, then there was room to negotiate a solution. All recognized that the "division" or "allocation" of share ownership had to go forward.

The reform started with a company in Hunan in 2005. The company was publicly traded with control shares held by privately-held capital. On April 29, 2005, the Board of Directors determined that out of a total of 240 million shares, each shareholder of 10 traded shares would receive 3 shares and eight RMB in cash. Shareholders of non-tradable shares would now have their shares become tradable and saleable on the stock market. This was an ice breaker. Since the deal was clinched at a low point in the markets, the reform went more smoothly than anyone expected. At the beginning of the "mobilization" of this reform, the stock market continued to decline for a while, going below the benchmark of 1000 in June. Once batch after batch of reform "test case" companies completed share-reform proceedings, however, the market began to stabilize. By September of 2006, 1,151 companies had already begun or completed procedures for share transformation. The percentage of

Left: September 28, 2005, the 2556th anniversary of the birth of Confucius. A ceremony was held to honor him at the Confucian Temple at Qufu, Shangdong Province. The revival of traditional culture has been seen as a mark of China's ascent.

Right: Ads everywhere, platering everything in sight.

reformed-share companies' market value to that of total market value gradually reached 92%. When most of the companies on the market had accomplished share reform, China's markets woke up suddenly from their bearish slumber.

In one important respect, the process of share-division reform was like the earlier "price-breaking-through-the-pass" reform of the late 1980s and the "enterprise-ownership-rights" reform of the late-1990s. It displayed the virtues of "no more debate." Every time a major reform in China was vigorously debated and forcefully proposed, it produced few results and was aborted. It even might have the negative effect of creating social discord and chaotic public opposition. When things had quieted down and all were exhausted, and the government indicated there was to be no more debate, reform was able to accomplish break-through progress.

In 2004, macro-economic measures were bringing deep-seated contradictions to the fore that pitted economic growth against systemic reform. The economist Wu Jinglian felt that China's reform was entering "the deep end of the pool." With each step forward, it was impinging upon the vested interests of some people or some Ministries. Further reforms encountered their stiff opposition. To many observers, the phrase "deep water" had many levels of implied meaning. It signified the ever greater difficulties of reform in the future, but also the unknown depths into which reform was plunging. It implied greater complexity and diversification of conflicts of interest. It meant that China was entering a vast, uncharted, totally unknown commercial era.

For many Chinese, the recent past is already a different country. In 2006, *Time* magazine published an issue with Mao Zedong on the cover. *Time* had put Chairman Mao on the cover six times, but this time he was wearing clothes with a Louis Vuitton logo, and the caption was the "Quiet Revolution."

On the high-speed superhighway of China's economic development, the privileged position of large State-owned enterprises was now becoming apparent. Their monopoly position in the realm of resources was being consolidated in an unprecedented way. If you were to think of China's economy

as a tree full of apples, then these companies were the recipient of all the apples from the biggest and most bountiful branches. Meanwhile, the competitiveness of these organizations was also being strengthened as their capital base became part of a market system. In the three years since the State-owned Assets Supervision and Commission of the State Council (SASAC) was established, income from the primary businesses of enterprises directly under the Central Government grew 78.8%, or an annual increase of 21.4%. Profits grew 140% or an annual increase of 33.8%. Tax revenue to the government increased 96.5%, or an annual increase of 25.2%. Net return on investment rate was 10%, increasing by 5% over the three years. The rate of what is called "preservation of State-owned assets" reached 144.4%. These State-owned industries and enterprises have truly become an invincible fleet.

Natural-resource industries will serve as a good example. China's three large monopoly oil companies enjoyed explosive profits in the years between 2004 and 2006, as resources became scarcer around the globe and the price of crude oil went from USD 25 to USD 70. China's three large oil companies are China Petroleum & Chemical Co. (also known as Sinopec), China National Petroleum Corp. (or CNPC, also known as Petro-China which is the traded arm of CNPC), and China National

November 5, 2007, PetroChina successfully listed its A shares on the stock market in Shanghai. Because of its monopoly advantage, the company became the 'most profitable company in all of Asia' in 2007.

Offshore Oil Corporation (or CNOOC). In 2004, the net profit of Sinopec grew 70% over the previous year. From this base, in 2005 net profit rose another 42% and in 2006 yet another 28.08%. PetroChina reported even more audacious figures. In 2005, it reported turnover of RMB 552.23 billion, an increase of 39% over the previous year. With net profits of RMB 133.36 billion, the company became the most profitable money-making machine in all of Asia. It surpassed the blue-chip king of the Hong Kong stock market, HSBC, and Asia's previously most-profitable company, Toyota.

In July 2006, *Fortune* magazine announced the names of the Global Fortune 500, and twenty-two Chinese companies were now on the list. Sinopec went from being #31 to #23, to stand as China's premier enterprise. The State Grid Corporation of China rose from #40 to stand at #32. PetroChina went from #46 to #39.

Similar things were happening in the financial arena. In May of 2006, the Construction Bank, Communications Bank, Bank of China, and Industrial and Commercial Bank of China were listed on exchanges and a portion of shares were taken public. Strategic international investors warmly received them. It is worth noting that those international financial institutions that stepped up briskly to climb onto the train were quickly able to reap tremendous returns. The listing and the profits made are events that are not likely to be repeated anytime soon.

By the end of 2006, a period of "macro-economic adjustments" that had extended for two years finally came to an end. In the past thirty years of reform processes, "macro-economic adjustments" had become a special noun in the Chinese vocabulary. This followed on its predecessor, "enforced reorganization," which was in vogue in the 1990s. Such "adjustments" now occurred with a regularity of every three to five years. The beginning was always trumpeted, but exactly when the adjustments were to end was never announced.

This time, the conclusion of the macro-economic adjustments could be recognized fairly clearly since the desired outcome had been achieved. Through strong-arm administrative

controls, the monopolistic position of State-owned enterprises in certain industries was strengthened.

Since 2006, merger-and-acquisition activity has clearly sped up. The listing of State-owned banks has been a major development. Two very large-scale projects were completed, while one has begun. On May 20, 2006, the final concrete was poured for the main wall of the Three Gorges Dam. Twelve years of construction required some USD 24 billion in investment up to that date. The dam was said to be able to put out 84.7 billion kwh of electricity on average per year, replacing Brazil's Itaipu dam as the world's largest flood-prevention and hydro-electric power project. On July 1, the Qinghai-Xizang (Tibet) Railway was completed. Extending 1,956 kilometers, the investment in this project came to RMB 33 billion. The railroad included 960 kilometers that were higher than 4,000 meters above sea level. It prided itself on being the highest and longest railroad in the world, built under the most extreme climatic conditions.

On June 6, the State Council issued an "Opinion regarding issues to do with opening a Tianjin Binhai New Area." The plan for this new region incorporated 2,270 square kilometers, which was 300 square kilometers bigger than Shenzhen, twice as big as Hong Kong, and three times as big as Pudong. Binhai New Area was to become the new financial center of the

Left: The Three Gorges dam is the largest engineering project ever undertaken by China. This photograph shows the moment an explosive charge explodes in the course of its construction.

Right: The Three Gorges Dam.

In 2007, the world's highest railroad in connected Qinghai and Xizang (Tibet). The photograph shows a representative piece of the extremely difficult engineering of the Qinghai-Tibet Railway, the Super-great Bridge at the Lhasa River. The three main arches symbolize the three white hatag. The Potala can be seen in Lhasa in the distance.

Tibetan antelopes running across the Qinghai-Tibet Railway.

northern part of China. People thought of it as the third in a succession of major development plans, after Shenzhen in the 1980s and Pudong in the 1990s. A Xinhua News Agency editorial applauded the news, "Shanghai's Pudong, Shenzhen City, and Tianjin's Binhai New Area are becoming the three engines in China's comprehensive reform."

On November 20, 2006, the Shanghai Exchange index broke through the benchmark figure of 2000, after being below it for six years. The index had fallen to 998.22 on June 6, 2005, to everyone's dismay. From January 2006, however, it began rising and in a short ten months the indicator surged 800 points, a rise of over 70%. After the completion of the Division of Shares Reform, the resurrection of the capital markets was very apparent and people began to take savings out of the bank and invest them in shares. In October, for the first time in five years, savings began to show a decline. The *Wall Street Journal* warned in an editorial, "China's rapid increase in foreign exchange reserves will lead to excess liquidity, which can lead to hyperinflation, an asset-pricing bubble, and the over-granting of loans by commercial

1. China's cities and their surroundings have become massive construction sites with increasing urbanization of the country. The two words 'chai qian' can be seen everywhere. Meaning, 'demolish, move,' they refer to demolition of older homes and people being moved elsewhere. Photographed in November 2007.

2. A shop being 'demolished and moved.'

3. A worker using a steel hammer to smash the remaining steel structure of a building.

4. A crane over buildings that are being levelled.

5. Workers retrieving steel beams that can be sold, from a building that has been demolished.

banks." Within half a year, these forebodings were all to come true.

Before that time, however, the recovery of the housing market was also clear-cut. After the macro-economic adjustments, real estate throughout the country stayed quiet but from the beginning of the year the markets in such cities as Beijing and Shanghai took the lead in rising again. The government attempted to keep down rising prices and, in order to keep the market in hand, issued one regulation that was of particular note: all residential construction that received permits after June 1, 2006, was supposed to put at least 70% of the construction costs into apartments that were 90 square meters or less. Clearly, this was a rule that nobody could conscientiously follow and it was never enforced. In the second half of the year, the central government continued to take restraining actions, banks raised interest rates, foreign money was forbidden to "flip" properties, and officials in some cities where housing prices rose too abruptly were disciplined. None of this had the slightest effect on the continuing rise in prices.

The rise in lock-step of both stock market prices and housing prices is generally a cardinal sign for a boom. It is an indicator of the start of another cycle of what could be called irrational prosperity.

Production line in Shanghai Volkswagon.

In China's case, the irrationality relates in part to factors that are not included in normal cost analysis, particularly environmental factors. There is no other country on earth quite like China as it is today, in that it seems to have left the confines of the real world, of the stability of things as they used to be. Most people look around and cannot detect any vestiges of the place where they grew up. Tang (618-907) and Song (960-1279) poetry depicts a landscape that is the opposite of what exists today. Foreigners know that China has become the manufacturing base for the world, but few people outside China know what that has

A worker in a shipbuilding factory in Dalian, Liaoning. Photographed in May 2007.

done to the land. The winding roads of olden days have been made into straight, uniform streets, lined with massive, monotonous concrete high rises. The flying eaves, bridges across streams, corridors around houses are images found in memory only. In the past twenty years, around 400 million people have been taken out of extreme poverty. This has been accomplished only as a result of extremely fast urbanization, and that has meant despoiling the land.

Experts are predicting that urbanization will continue. In the coming twenty years, another 400 million people are expected to move into cities. All of China is a massive construction site. The following statistics give some idea of what kind of place the country has become. The area under construction every day in China equals roughly half of the

Car exhibition. Photographed in Xi'an, Shaanxi, in 2008.

total new construction underway on any given day around the world. Only one year's worth of construction in China is roughly equivalent to the total amount of existing construction in Russia today. The result of only ten days of construction in the city of Chongqing is equivalent to the building of fifteen new Chrysler Buildings in New York. To repeat, fifteen new Chrysler Buildings in just ten days, and in just one city.

In the summer of 2006, a film called *Still Life* by the young film director Jia Zhangke won the Golden Lion Award at the Venice Film Festival. Its Chinese name means "Three Gorges' Nice Men." The footage was filmed in Fengjie County near Chongqing, which has enjoyed over two thousand years of history. In five months of filming, Jia discovered that his camera could not keep up with the changing scene. An old historic tower in the distance was there at the start, but gone by the time he had made a trip to Beijing and come back. Within the circumference of his lens, everything was changed, buildings, landscape, daily life. In five months, reality was changed.

The bestseller called *The World is Flat* has been popular in China and become a topic of everyone's conversation. In this book, the author declares that things like the fall of the Berlin Wall, the rise of the Internet, and the activity of Open Source have flattened the global, political, economic, and cultural scene, so that people who previously had no access to power and wealth can now directly participate in making money and in creating public policy. All they need is patience, some creativity, and broadband access.

Americans and Chinese may read this evaluation of the world in different ways. Americans may feel that they are in the process of flattening the world. Many Chinese firmly believe that they are in the process of moving from the edges of the world towards the center of a world that has already largely been "crushed flat." This is a reflection of what they see immediately around them.

Jack Ma (Ma Yun) motivating his staff. The Internet became fertile ground for the birth of China's new-style companies.

Internet Economics

On November 6, 2007, a company called Alibaba was listed on the Hong Kong stock exchange. Its helmsman, Ma Yun, or, in English, Jack Ma, is known for his mischievous smile and his fondness for saying shocking things. Ma heads an internet services company that provides a foreign trade platform to six million small and medium-sized enterprises. The Hong Kong listing was highly successful. Twelve years earlier, Ma had been a foreign language teacher in a very ordinary college in Hangzhou when, as they say in China, he began to "draw a tiger by looking at a cat." Without knowing anything about the real thing, since it did not exist in China, he began to make a Chinese-language webpage.

Jack Ma (Ma Yun), founder of the e-commerce company, Alibaba, was put on the cover of Forbes magazine at a time when his small company was still operating out of an apartment in Hangzhou.

The placard for one of China's earliest internet companies, Info Highway: 'How far is China from the information highway of the Internet?'

Alibaba is an unimaginable super-fairytale to many people. From the shares allotted to foreign investors, Alibaba received subscriptions of USD 180 billion since the offering was approximately 186 times over-subscribed. This broke all records at the Hong Kong exchange. The wild scene made the *Economist* wonder, "Is Alibaba the start of a China.com bubble?"

One thinks back to the winter of 1995, when a sign was set out on the street in Beijing's Zhongguancun that read: "How far from the Information Highway are Chinese? Go 1,500 meters to the north." At the time many people took this to be a road sign. They thought that policemen had put it there. When people finally realized that it referred to the Chinese internet, this first mention of the Internet became a kind of milestone, marking a certain stage in China's development. Alibaba's listing in Hong Kong became another milestone: the road in between had taken a mere twelve years.

That road was paved with the efforts of a number of superlative entrepreneurs. Three young people were to appear collectively in China, in 1997, to declare that the Founding year of China's internet had arrived. One was Ding Lei, another was Wang Zhidong, and the third was Zhang Chaoyang.

Ding Lei, or William Ding, founded a company called NetEase in Guangzhou, Guangdong. His slogan was, "network everyone's powers," and at the beginning his plan was very simple. If people wanted to use the Internet to communicate with one another, they needed their own "room," or "mailbox." So he wrote the first Chinese-language individual homepage service system, and combined it with a free mailbox system. He did not pay too much attention to the financial aspect, of how NetEase was going to make money. The reason was that business models were always changing and he couldn't think clearly about it. Even less could he imagine that, six years later, he would become the richest person in China.

In Beijing, a young software engineer named Wang Zhidong was able to get funding from an American venture capital firm, which was the first Chinese internet company to be funded in this way. When he first set up his website, he posted a number of special forums, and discovered to his surprise that the response to technology forum was lukewarm while the response to the sports forum was red hot. On October 31, China's soccer team participated in the World Cup's tenth competition in Asia, held at the Jinzhou Stadium in Dalian. China lost to a small oil-rich country named Qatar that has a population of only 520,000. At 2:15 am the next morning, a Net-friend named Lao Rong sent out a message to the sports salon saying, "No tears at Dalian's Jinzhou." Within forty-eight hours, this had received twenty thousand hits and become the first internet article to get mass attention. The grassroots nature of the internet and its astonishing ability to transmit information were for the first time realized in China. Wang Zhidong's forum was later to become the influential and powerful news portal called Sina.

Zhang Chaoyang, or Charles Zhang, a graduate of MIT in Boston, also started a website in 1997. He called it Sohu. He received USD 225,000 in start-up capital from two American professors, one of whom was the guru of the digital age, Nicholas Negroponte. When the website first started it had no content so he simply put Negroponte's book, *Being Digital*, up there. He too had little idea how he was going to make money. Later, when the initial investment was all spent, he sat on pins and needles until he was able to get USD 2.15 million in investment

The Boao Forum, held once a year, has become one of the most important non-governmental forums in Asia. This photographs shows Microsoft's Chairman of the Board, Bill Gates, at the opening ceremonies in April 2007.

from Intel and Dow Jones. As the "Chinese representative," he was included in *Time* magazine's "Fifty Global Digital Heroes," and subsequently became the first of China's internet-economy heroes.

In 1999, Sina chose the famous international investment group Morgan Stanley to be its partner in going public. Morgan Stanley was a great investment firm, but it had little understanding of the internet, especially since this was a *Chinese* internet company. All Morgan Stanley knew was that this was definitely going to be a business in which one could make major money. In the negotiations, Sina noted that the strategic direction of the future would be to set up a "portal website." Morgan Stanley's senior officer lowered his head and said sideways to the man in charge of the project, "I always thought Sina was an internet company. What do they want a door for?" He had not yet learned the difference between a "door" and a "portal," but his enthusiasm for China internet continued just the same. In 1997, all three large portal websites, Sina, NetEase, and Sohu, were listed with brilliant results on Nasdaq.

These internet companies and others were still dreaming sweet dreams when a blast of winter blew in. In April of 1998, the Nasdaq in America suddenly turned and within half a year its index dropped by 40%. USD 8.5 trillion of market value evaporated. All the main internet companies were in trouble and the several Chinese companies that had listed in America were not immune to the general decline. Sina.com's shares dropped to a low of USD 1.06; Sohu.com dropped to USD 0.60, NetEase was even worse, with its share price going to a mere USD 0.53. The tender young Chinese internet economy fell into a chasm from which no more bubbles were to emerge for some time.

The worst of all was NetEase. At one point in 2001, trading in the shares was stopped due to financial disclosure problems. Ding Lei was remembering those times when he said, "At the time I was very conflicted and even thought of selling NetEase at one point. The reason I didn't sell is not that I wouldn't sell, but that our audit had problems and people weren't willing to buy." Even with his back to the wall, Ding Lei quickly began to sniff out where opportunities might lie. He soon announced that he was investing in an internet game called "Journey to the West," since a movie of the same name was well received by college students at the time. He also developed a "sms" service together with mobile telephone companies. Although he lost another RMB 200 million that year, the internet game and the sms business saved this young man. He was later to say in a speech to college students, "Before I turned thirty, my biggest achievement was not that I had made two or three hundred million RMB, but that I had gained the experience of losing two or three hundred million."

It was a tough time. The internet economy had happily overturned the old business models of corporate growth and the old rules of wealth accumulation, but in the ten years to come, eternal business laws were to reassert themselves, often in a most tragic and direct way. They confirmed that all those who want to succeed must, as always, pass through the fire. Crisis is the best teacher but for many the hardship was worth the end result. After two years of little action, the geyser-like era of the Internet started spouting again. Just as many of China's enterprises were facing SARS and other problems, China's internet economy began to reappear in embryonic form.

On October 10, 2003, the share price of NetEase hit USD

70.27, its historic high. This was a rise of 617% over the company's price at the beginning of the year, and it was 108 times the price on September 1, 2001. Ding Lei's wealth on paper now exceeded RMB 5 billion, making him the first Chinese internet entrepreneur to become the richest person in China. This quantifying of wealth shone a very stark light on the new business reality: not only was wealth able to be generated in a very short time, but young progressive entrepreneurs had become a major force in business. Power equations in China had shifted.

Alibaba exemplified this in the realm of e-commerce. The appearance of SARS in early 2003 had put this company through a severe test. An Alibaba employee attended the Canton (Guangzhou) Fair as part of her business responsibilities, only to discover on return that she had contracted SARS. All five hundred employees in Alibaba were immediately quarantined and normal operations of the company were shut down. Everyone had to work from home. Paradoxically, this proved a turning point in China in awareness of the merits of e-commerce. Normal business in China requires face-to-face meetings, generally in the context of a meal. Since this was suddenly impossible, many enterprises began to rely on the Internet to sustain contact and look for business. Alibaba's volume increased and the company became China's largest internet company in the space of four years.

In May of 2004, thirty-some-year-old Chen Tianqiao took his company, Shanda Interactive Entertainment, public on Nasdaq in America. Within the space of one night he too became one the richest people in China, after which he went through the amusing act of buying Sina. Yet it had only been a few years earlier, in 1999, that he had quit his job and rented three small rooms in Pudong where he developed a graphic interface internet game. It was not well received, but by agenting the Korean game called "The Legend of Mir," his company was able to make so much money that the market value of Shanda shares reached USD 3.5 billion. His own personal wealth reached RMB 9 billion. The whole process took less than five years.

Baidu was another success story, and one that employed

uniquely Chinese strategy. The global king in the realm of search engines was Google, which in China looked like a rare imported orchid next to the "weedy" look of Baidu. What Baidu soon did, however, was to rank names according to a competitive pricing system. This aimed at small and medium-sized companies as the source of profits. All you had to do was pay a few hundred RMB in advance and you would be allowed to have your company bumped up to the head of the list when the search engine displayed search results to a potential customer. The service was somewhere in between advertising and e-commerce, and for Baidu it flung open the doors to profit. Baidu listed on Nasdaq in August 2005, which started a crazy wave of overseas IPO of Chinese internet companies.

In the past fifteen years, the internet in China has grown wildly from a starting point of zero. Not only has the internet formed a real industry, but it has penetrated every crack, every cell of economic life in the country. Chinese are quite proud

The internet has enabled the next generation of young people in China to become a globalized generation. They connect in a seamless and natural way with the world. Photographed in an Internet bar in November, 2007.

of this industry for one special reason: unlike other industries, this one has allowed local Chinese to compete successfully against international competition. Even a behemoth like Google is not exempt from the challenge: it has less than half of Baidu's market in China. Another feature of China's internet scene is that most companies purchased by overseas investors have run into problems. In the search engine field, "3721" ceased to exist after being bought by Yahoo. Joyo, in the B2C business, sank into a torpor after being purchased by Amazon. EachNet, after being bought by eBay, ran into the frontal attack of Alibaba's Taobao.

The internet seems to create miracles. It is like a big kiln that can produce ceramics of incomparable beauty, but only after the pot has been seared in flames. It gives one hope for China's future, for this industry did not exist when reform and opening up began. The "Me Generation" (children born after 1980), following on the generation who started their internet businesses, now begin their own stories. Young people are now overturning the very way business is done. They are a generation born into a globalized world. They regard the internet as a seamless part of their daily lives. They grew up in households and in a society that was already "open;" they did not go through the debilitating and disfiguring scorching of ideology. They escaped traditional restraints, especially the burden of an ownership system that was partially held by the State. They have been more fortunate than business people in any former generation. If China is to bring forth a great company that is world-class, and Chinese entrepreneurs that are worthy of being world-famous, it may well be that these companies and entrepreneurs will come from the realm of the internet.

Before the Olympic 'Bird's Nest' in Beijing. A new couple wearing old-styled clothes have their photograph taken while peasant workers surround them to watch. A 'changing China' can be glimpsed in this photograph.

Great Nation Passion

CCTV broadcast a television show in the spring of 2007 that was called "The Rise of the Great Powers," and it drew a tremendous audience.

The show discussed the evolution of nine great nations in the world, over the past five hundred years. China was not included among them. CCTV did no special advertising for this show, and did not air it on prime time but the program became the most hotly debated subject in intellectual circles and on the internet. An unprecedented "Great Nation Passion" seemed to have struck a chord in everyone.

In many ways, "Chinese-ness" was now very much in fashion. At the beginning of 2007, many economists were predicting that China's GDP would surpass that of Germany, making China the third largest economic entity in the world after America and Japan. People began to feel more self-confident. Traditional culture became newly in vogue. A show called "Experts' forum" that discussed traditional Chinese culture became the most popular late-night show on television. Two professors talked about such things as the *Three Kingdoms* and the *Analects of Confucius* and were instantly the rage. Their books were always placed in a prime spot in bookstores, and wherever they went they were mobbed like movie stars. S.H.E., a popular girls' singing group in Taiwan, used a song called *Chinese Language* as the theme song of their new annual disc. "The whole world is talking Chinese," went the lyrics, "and what we Chinese are saying now has to be heard by the rest of the world."

The Chinese stock market meanwhile entered a kind of "mass mania." Within the space of half a year, shares surged upwards. PE ratios were as high as fifty or sixty, in some cases one hundred up to one thousand. Every day, some 300,000 new stock accounts were opened. These people included not only white-collar urban residents, old hands at managing money, but also college students, farmers, petty traders, anyone's neighbor. The pawn-shop business was thriving. Many people pawned their house to the bank and then charged into the market. They may not have ever heard of a PE ratio. One shareholder created a song on the Internet, "I'll hold on till I'm dead, I won't sell," which became the ring tone on many people's cell phones. The song went, "Won't be happy till my shares have doubled, won't sell till they do," and so on. By May 25, the number of accounts opened via the exchange companies at the Shanghai and Shenzhen exchanges had broken through the 100 million mark.

If the stock market craze had reached a high fever, the craze in housing prices and the stories of sudden wealth were stupefying.

Housing prices had doubled in many cities, even tripled. Given the approaching 2008 Olympics, Beijing prices were skyrocketing, going up every week. You could not find anything for less than RMB 10,000 per square meter within the Fifth Ring Road, and even at that price, supply could not meet demand. Buyers stood in line all night waiting to buy houses, afraid that in this lifetime they would not be able to get into the market otherwise. One developer told a journalist that he was getting embarrassed at the profits he was making. This continued until the government put emergency measures in place by issuing a whole series of financial tightening measures. At the same time it released cheaper housing and cheaper rental housing onto the market, which brought the prices down somewhat.

Just as the geyser was erupting in the shares and the housing markets, an unexpected thing occurred. On "May 1st" this year, so-called Golden Week in China when everyone takes a vacation, tourists strolling around Lake Taihu noticed a sort of green-ness floating on the lake in many areas. In some places it was so thick that it looked like a layer of paint. In other areas, large numbers of dead fish were floating belly up. Experts explained that this had been caused by the eruption of a blue algae bloom. Due to this blue algae bloom, the water quality of Wuxi City and other parts of Jiangsu Province suddenly worsened. It began to stink. It could not be used for drinking and there was suddenly a run on the purefied water in supermarkets.

This blue algae incident shocked the entire country. Chemical industries are situated all along the banks of Lake Taihu. Their discharge of waste water had never been adequately regulated or controlled so that Taihu's water became severely eutrophied. It contained ten times the standard amount of nitrogen and phosphorus. In just the past two years, both industrial discharge and discharged of wastewater from residents around Taihu had put an estimated 5.3 billion tons of wastewater into the lake. Only 30% of water flowing into the lake had undergone water treatment so that pollutants far exceeded the carrying capacity of the water environment of the region.

China's pollution problems have become of general concern around the world. A World Bank report noted that sixteen of the globe's twenty most heavily polluted cities are in China. *Newsweek* published an article called, "China Exports Pollution." The reporter noted, "In recent years, the air in Beijing has become as thick as that particularly viscous kind of egg-drop soup. 'Made in China' implies cheap shoddy goods, but

GLOSSARY

Wu-yi

Or May 1, was a traditional time of holiday celebrations in China. In 1999, the government issued regulations that increased the number of legally determined holidays for the public. Spring Festival (Chinese New Year), May 1 (Labor Day) and October 1 (National Day) were all designated as three-day holidays, in addition to the days before and after that could be taken as holidays. Every year carried the possibility of three seven-day-long holiday periods. Because of the traveling and the resulting consumer spending, they became known as Golden Weeks. One of the motivations for having Golden Weeks was the impact of the Asian financial crisis in 1998. The government wanted to stimulate consumption and help the domestic economy. Starting in 2008, the May 1 Golden Week holiday has been eliminated: 2007 was the last time for this holiday.

Taxi drivers are taking English lessons for the coming Olympic Games. Photographed in Beijing, April 2007.

now the country is exporting something far more expensive: environmental degradation. Acid rain and other pollutants are already poisoning close to one-quarter of China's tillable land. Some regions of Japan and Korea are experiencing the withering of crops due to China's acid rain. Over-felling of trees and destruction of grasslands is leading to violently fast desertification in China's northern tier, to the extent that wind-blown sand is reaching the west coast of America. Right now, 27% of China's land is undergoing desertification. America pumps more greenhouse gasses into the air than any other country on earth, but China is a close second. It has become the globe's second worst source of pollution."

Environmental degradation is a heavy price to pay for economic advancement. The subject has become one of high concern to both the world and to citizens of China. According to professional estimates, China's GDP occupies 5.5% of the gross product of the world, but its consumption of resources is shockingly higher. China consumes 8% of the world's consumption of oil, 40% of raw coal, 32% of crude steel, 25% of aluminum oxide, 48% of cement, 33% of glass, and 30% of fertilizers. China's reliance on foreign mining sources for its resources has gone from 5% in 1990 to over 50% in 2007. At the same time, the efficiency with which China uses resources is low. All indicators show that China is using resources at an astonishing rate for a number of reasons, and clearly at a rate that will be impossible to sustain.

In the fall of 2007, China's National Development and Reform Commission arranged for RMB 540 million of government bonds to support ninety-eight resource-conserving projects. The State Council also signed off on forty-five resource-conserving targets for central key industries. A new "resource conservation law" is soon to be put forth.

At the same time, the verbal international attacks aimed at "Made in China" have intensified, and censure of "Made in China" has become a tool that politicians can reach for at any time. A *Financial Times'* reporter based in Beijing describes the contradictory attitude in the West as follows, "On the one hand, Western consumers are deriving great benefit [from cheap goods], on the other hand, they are complaining loudly about shoddy goods and saying that they are losing jobs in their local regions while allowing China to gain undeniable benefit."

In fact, as the RMB has continued to appreciate, and as international businesses are entering and competing inside China, many enterprises in China are already turning towards their own domestic market. In July of 2007, China's largest sock manufacturer, the Langsha Group, announced that at the end of the month it would be handing over the last batch of goods and would no longer be taking any orders from Wal-Mart. This company had sold USD 5 million worth of products to Wal-Mart every year, but the profit margins were too slim and it was finally time to let go.

Another constantly increasing pressure on Chinese enterprises is the growing rate of inflation inside China. The price advantage of "Made in China" has been declining, but it should be noted that this is not just a domestic China

A cement factory along the banks of the Wujiang River has destroyed the beautiful scenery, because of severe pollution from emissions. Photographed in April 2005.

'Water Cube'—the Beijing National Aquatics Center. Photographed in May 2008.

problem. Since China is indeed supplier to the world, the rest of the world's prices are impacted. The U.S. Commerce Department indicated that in the first half of 2007, prices on imports from China had already risen 4.1%. This was the fastest change since America started to track China-import prices in 2003 and it was much higher than the 2% inflation in America overall. A China analyst at the Royal Bank of Scotland explained, succinctly, "In the past ten years, China was a force for deflation, but in the coming ten years, it will be a force for inflation."

In *The Age of Turbulence: Adventures in a New World*, the former Chairman of the Federal Reserve Alan Greenspan voiced similar concerns. He described the international scene as follows. Among old-style powers in Europe, England was best situated for growth. With its strong natural-resource base, Russia would also move forward. India had the most potential in its heavy industries and its IT service industries, while Japan, albeit still in a slump, would retain its "great strength." While expressing concern about the American economy, Greenspan predicted that, in 2030, China would become America's main competitor. He said, "The way in which China moves forward to embrace global markets will determine the fate of the economies of the entire globe."

China seems to be operating under two scenarios as it approaches the Olympics and thereafter. On the one hand, Chinese have the sense that a massive force is ascending and the influence of China is increasing daily. On the other hand, the stock markets are erratic, the real estate market is falling, the RMB continues to appreciate and CPI remains high. How these two scenarios intersect and play into the future is a major cause for both concern and ongoing debate.

The May 2007 issue of the *Economist* carried on its cover a picture of "King Kong" climbing the Empire State Building, clutching a panda. This was reminiscent of another cover back in 1989: Sony had just purchased Columbia Pictures, and *Newsweek* ran a cover with the Statue of Liberty wearing a kimono. Just one year later, however, the Japanese stock market had plunged, the real estate bubble had burst, and the Japanese economy had fallen into a pit from which it has taken seventeen long years to emerge. Will China follow the same course? Everything seems to depend on people's attitude and their intelligence. An exciting era is quickly retreating into the distance for China. As a major nation that is in the process of peaceful ascendance, China is beginning a long, hard, reason-based trek.

Left: 'Panda Climbs the Empire State Building' announced the cover of the *Economist* in May, 2007. The image was of King Kong ascending the building with a panda clutched to his chest. It reminded many Chinese of that famous cover eighteen years earlier, when *Newsweek* clothed the Statue of Liberty in a kimono.

Right: In 1989, the Japanese economy was at its height, Sony had just bought Columbia Pictures, and *Newsweek* put the kimono-clad Statue of Liberty on its cover. The Japanese miracle lasted until May of 1990, when the bubble burst. The Tokyo Stock Exchange plummeted, real estate prices collapsed, and Japan entered a 17-year-long period of economic stagnation.

The new CCTV building in Beijing, under construction, a surreal and ultra-modern building.

Crossroads

History is like that two-faced Janus of ancient Roman my-thology: one face gazes backwards while the other stares intently into the future.

Looking back to 1978, we see a country that was standing to one side of the world, solitary and traveling along its own course. Prolonged political struggle had made its people anxious and apathetic about the future. Any individual vitality was suffocated. At the beginning of the opening of the country, both leaders and the common man seemed to feel helpless in the face of the enormity of the problems. There could be no assistance from outside. At the same time, internal resources were exhausted and a rigid system bound the hands and feet of absolutely everyone.

Now, thirty years later, a paralyzed planned-economy system has gradually been disassembled. A group of ordinary people, unreconciled to their apparent destinies, took matters in their own hands. "Small people," they turned a "huge country" of 1.3 billion people into one vast experiment. Under the astonished gaze of everyone, knowing they were unable to turn back, they turned China in the direction of a commercial

The southern part of China encountered rare blizzards just around the time of Chinese New Year, 2008. The photograph shows peasant workers who are unable to return home due to the weather.

society and in the direction of the outside world. In order to pursue individual self-determination and well being, China's people managed to join the main current of history. Just as Premier Wen Jiabao has said, "China owes all this progress to the policy of reform and opening up and, in the final analysis, to the freedom-inspired creativity of the Chinese people." From the longer historical perspective, the period from 1978 to 2008 in China is going to be an epoch that can never be repeated.

Over the course of these past thirty years, people have continued to debate "is it called socialism or capitalism." They keep at it until their faces are blue and their very ears turn red. At the beginning, risk-takers paid a heavy price for this, but it was exactly this kind of debate that impelled China's rise. The debate is based on believing in actual results. Unlike the reform in Eastern European socialist countries, China chose an extremely unusual path of gradual reform. There has been no lack of difficulties and conflicts, but facts seem to indicate that this was the correct path to the future.

Along the course of this oft-changing extraordinary process, even up to today, people have not been able to discern what economists blithely refer to as "objective laws." In a certain sense, the thirty years of the Chinese economic miracle has represented the victory of the purest experimentalism, of a

Upper: The strongest earthquake in China in more than thirty years occurred on May 12, 2008, in Wenchuan, Sichuan. Almost 90,000 died or disappeared and China's society faced a tough public test in dealing with the calamity. Photo shows rubble after the earthquake in Beichuan's county seat.

Middle: Earthquake relief. On May 17, 2008, Chinese army and air force representatives traveled deep into mountainous regions to administer emergency relief and to transport the heavily wounded from Mianzhu City into Qingping County.

Lower: People praying, photographed on May 19, 2008, the first of the National Days of Mourning.

very practical and concrete approach to events. To take leave of extreme poverty and to try to modernize—these have been the over-riding desire of both people and government. So long as people could "feel for the stones with their feet as they crossed the river," so long as they knew that irrespective of whether you were a white cat or a black cat, so long as you caught mice you knew you were a good cat, they could face any setbacks. The truth had tens of thousands of different aspects. Development was a tough road, with curves and switchbacks, but it was the right road.

The China of 2008 stands again at a crossroads. It may be that the questions will only be answered by history: where is the country going, what future setbacks will it be encountering. After the Olympics, China will celebrate the sixtieth anniversary of the founding of the People's Republic of China, and Shanghai will host the World Expo in 2010. There is no indication at this point that all the fine prospects ahead will not be fulfilled. At the same time, inflationary pressures are not abating, Made-in-China is being forced to change its tune, environmental problems become more pronounced by the day, and the directions of political reform and the implementation of a "harmonious society" are very unclear.

It may be that all of what has come before has just been a transient test. At this moment, what people need to be thinking about may be something quite different. China's past thirty years have to be unprecedented in history as the revival of a

1. The Great Wenchuan earthquake was the most severe earthquake in China since the Tangshan Earthquake of 1976. In this photograph, people light candles before the Tangshan Memorial, praying for people caught in the Wenchuan disaster.

2. The National Theater. Photographed in March 2008.

3. The Bird's Nest. Photographed in March 2008.

2

people: have we prepared psy-chologically during this pell-mell process? Have we done adequate ethical preparation in meeting the rise of commercial prosperity? Will we sink into self-adulation? Have we learned adequately how to play the role of a great power? World-class prestige and world-class risk co-exist in China's economy, like inseparable twins who will both affect the future. As we move towards an unfathom-able tomorrow, we must maintain a necessary sense of alertness, not because we are afraid but because the willingness to question and to debate represents a maturing un-derstanding of how we cultivate who we want to be.

3

Acknowledgments

A competition among China's photographers was held to provide historical as well as contemporary photographs to help document this book. We would like to thank those whose lenses participated in recording history. They include: An Ge, Bao Kun, Chen Shaohua, Chen Xiaobo, Deng Wei, Geng Zhigang, Fu Xiaoming, Gu Zheng, He Yanguang, Hu Wugong, Hu Ying, Huang Wen, Huang Xin, Huo Wei, Le Yi, Li Ge, Li Mei, Li Shufeng, Li Yanhong, Liu Jie, Liu Shuyong, Lü Xiang, Meng Renquan, Qiu Huining, Qiu Xianglin, Ruan Xiao, Sheng Xigui, Si Sushi, Su Zhigang, Sun Jingtao, Tan Chengfa, Wang Jingchun, Wang Qian, Wang Wenlan, Wang Yao, Wu Hongze, Xia Donghai, Xie Qingsong, Xu Huading, Yang Dejun, Yang Zhitao, Ye Chao, Ye Zhiwen, Yong He, Yu Wenguo, Yuan Yun, Zeng Huang, Zhang Guangyuan, Zhang Tao, Zhang Xiangdong, Zhang Xiaonian, Zhang Xinmin, and Zhuang Rungui. Their names are listed in alphabetical order by surname.

Renmin University of China
Sohu.com
Wu Xiaobo
June, 2008